Ralph Ellison's
INVISIBLE MAN

A CONTEMPORARY
LITERARY VIEWS BOOK

Edited and with an Introduction by
HAROLD BLOOM

© 1996 by Chelsea House Publishers, a division of Main Line Book Co.

Introduction © 1996 by Harold Bloom

Printed and bound in the United States of America.

First Printing
1 3 5 7 9 8 6 4 2

Cover illustration: UPI/Bettmann Newsphotos

Library of Congress Cataloging-in-Publication Data

Ralph Ellison's Invisible man / edited and with an introduction by Harold Bloom.
p. cm. — (Bloom's Notes)
Includes bibliographical references and index.
Summary: Includes a brief biography of the author, thematic and structural analysis of the work, critical views, and an index of themes and ideas.
ISBN 0-7910-4062-3
1. Ellison, Ralph. Invisible man. 2. Afro-American men in literature.
3. Afro-Americans in literature. [1. Ellison, Ralph. Invisible man. 2. American literature—History and criticism.] I. Bloom, Harold. II. Series.
PS3555.L62515 1995b
813'.54—dc20
95-45116
CIP
AC

Chelsea House Publishers
1974 Sproul Road, Suite 400
P.O. Box 914
Broomall, PA 19008-0914

Contents

User's Guide

This volume is designed to present biographical, critical, and bibliographical information on Ralph Ellison and *Invisible Man*. Following Harold Bloom's introduction, there appears a detailed biography of the author, discussing the major events in his life and his important literary works. Then follows a thematic and structural analysis of the work, in which significant themes, patterns, and motifs are traced. An annotated list of characters supplies brief information on the chief characters in the work.

A selection of critical extracts, derived from previously published material by leading critics, then follows. The extracts consist of such things as statements by the author on his work, early reviews of the work, and later evaluations down to the present day. The items are arranged chronologically by date of first publication. A bibliography of Ellison's writings (including a complete listing of books he wrote, cowrote, edited, or translated, along with important posthumous publications), a list of additional books and articles on him and on *Invisible Man,* and an index of themes and ideas conclude the volume.

Harold Bloom is Sterling Professor of the Humanities at Yale University and Henry W. and Albert A. Berg Professor of English at the New York University Graduate School. He is the author of twenty books and the editor of more than thirty anthologies of literature and literary criticism.

Professor Bloom's works include *Shelley's Mythmaking* (1959), *The Visionary Company* (1961), *Blake's Apocalypse* (1963), *Yeats* (1970), *A Map of Misreading* (1975), *Kabbalah and Criticism* (1975), and *Agon: Towards a Theory of Revisionism* (1982). *The Anxiety of Influence* (1973) sets forth Professor Bloom's provocative theory of the literary relationships between the great writers and their predecessors. His most recent books are *The American Religion* (1992) and *The Western Canon* (1994).

Professor Bloom earned his Ph.D. from Yale University in 1955 and has served on the Yale faculty since then. He is a 1985 MacArthur Foundation Award recipient and served as the Charles Eliot Norton Professor of Poetry at Harvard University in 1987–88. He is currently the editor of the Chelsea House series Major Literary Characters and Modern Critical Views, and other Chelsea House series in literary criticism.

Introduction

HAROLD BLOOM

I have argued elsewhere that the late Ralph Waldo Ellison's *Invisible Man* represents the outstanding African-American achievement in the arts to date, except for the musical accomplishments of Louis Armstrong, Charlie Parker, and Bud Powell. At once comic and tragic, and alas still prophetic, *Invisible Man* competes with the work of Thomas Pynchon and Philip Roth as the most distinguished American prose fiction since the death of William Faulkner. The imaginative wealth of Ellison's only published novel seems inexhaustible; fresh insights become apparent with each rereading. At once naturalistic, impressionist-symbolic, and surrealistic, the book ends in a mode of irrealism, pioneering a style exploited by Pynchon in *Gravity's Rainbow.* Like his namesake Emerson, Ellison was both a transcendentalist and a pragmatist, and again like Emerson, he firmly resisted the apocalyptic temptation. Fleeing both the Brotherhood (the Communist party) and Ras the Exhorter (a forerunner of the younger Malcolm X and Farrakhan), the Invisible Man goes underground, to cultivate an ultimate self-reliance, illuminated by 1,369 old-fashioned filament lightbulbs, which he enjoys while refusing to pay tribute to Monopolated Light & Power (Consolidated Edison).

The African-American critic Robert B. Stepto has identified in Ellison's novel, as elsewhere in black fiction, "the narratives of ascent and immersion." In Douglas Robinson's development of these movements, they come together as "the Jonah motif." Following Father Mapple's great sermon on Jonah in Melville's *Moby-Dick,* Ellison has his Invisible Man listen to a record of Louis Armstrong, greatest genius of jazz, singing and playing "What Did I Do to Be So Black and Blue." Within Armstrong's music, in a visionary breakthrough, Ellison's hero hears another music, in which a preacher and congregation exchange answers, and the preacher cries out: "It'll put you, glory, glory, Oh my Lawd, in the WHALE'S BELLY." Jonah, a failed prophet, is also a survivor, and so is the nameless Invisible Man, Ellison's equivalent of Melville's Ishmael, the narrator of *Moby-Dick.*

Weary of being a phantom in the mind of other people, white *and* black, the Invisible Man survives underground in the whale's belly, augmenting his sense of self and perfecting an image of voice that can speak universally.

Ellison was a great artist, not a social activist, and he suffered much abuse from those who felt he was not revolutionary or separatist enough. He wisely declined to compromise his mastery of the art of fiction by becoming the novelist version either of Ras the Exhorter, whole-hearted but doom-eager, or the sinister Rinehart, reverend and runner, both of whom have their mock-aesthetic equivalents. T. S. Eliot and Joseph Conrad mattered greatly to his writing, and so did Louis Armstrong and Charlie Parker. The humor, the pathos, the invention of *Invisible Man* manifest themselves upon the highest level of American fiction. Lurking in the book, underground with its protagonist, is a tragedy, not so much of the African Americans but of most Americans of good will, of whatever lineage. Call it the social tragedy of the United States of America, already two nations if not more, and being driven towards despair and violence by the emancipation of selfishness that belongs to the political age that goes from Reagan to Gingrich and beyond. ✤

Biography of Ralph Ellison

Ralph Waldo Ellison was born on March 1, 1914, in Oklahoma City, Oklahoma. His father, Lewis Ellison, was a construction worker and tradesman who died when Ellison was three. His mother, Ida Millsap, worked as a domestic servant but was active in radical politics for many years. Ellison thrived on the discarded magazines and phonograph records she brought home from the white households where she worked. He attended Douglass High School in Oklahoma City, where he learned the soprano saxophone, trumpet, and other instruments, playing both jazz and light classical music.

In 1933 Ellison began studying music at the Tuskegee Institute in Alabama. He remained there for three years before coming to New York in 1936, where he held a number of odd jobs while continuing to study music and sculpture. In New York he met Langston Hughes and Richard Wright, who gave him great encouragement in his writing. Ellison's short stories, essays, and reviews began appearing in the *Antioch Review,* the *New Masses,* and many other magazines and journals in the late 1930s. At this time his interest in social justice attracted him to the Communist party, although he would later repudiate it. Ellison gained a modicum of financial security in 1938 when he was hired by the Federal Writers' Project to gather folklore and present it in literary form. The four years he spent at this work enriched his own writing by providing source material that would be incorporated into his own fiction.

In 1943, wishing to help in the war effort, Ellison joined the merchant marine. The next year he received a Rosenwald Foundation Fellowship to write a novel; although he mapped out a plot, he failed to finish the work (one section was published as a short story, "Flying Home"). After the war he went to a friend's farm in Vermont to recuperate, and it was here that he conceived the novel that would establish him as a major writer—*Invisible Man.* He worked on the book for five years, and it was finally published in 1952. This long novel is both a historical biography of the black man in America and an allegory of man's quest for identity. *Invisible Man* received the National Book Award for fiction in 1953 and is now regarded as one of the most distinguished American novels of the century. *Shadow and Act* (1964), Ellison's second book, is a collection of personal essays about literature, folklore, jazz, and the author's life.

Even before finishing *Invisible Man,* Ellison had conceived the idea for another novel. Although he published several segments of it as short stories and read others on television and at lectures, the work remained unfinished at the time of his death; a large portion of it was destroyed by a fire at Ellison's summer home in Massachusetts in 1967. Because he did not advocate black separatism, Ellison fell out of sympathy with the black writers and thinkers of the 1960s; but over the last two decades he again became a much sought-after lecturer on college campuses. A second collection of essays, *Going to the Territory,* was published in 1986.

Ralph Ellison held visiting professorships at Yale, Bard College, the University of Chicago, and elsewhere. From 1970 to 1979 he was Albert Schweitzer Professor in the Humanities at New York University, later becoming an emeritus professor there. He held a fellowship of the American Academy of Arts and Letters in Rome from 1955 to 1957 and received the United States Medal of Freedom in 1969. He was a charter member of the National Council of the Arts, served as trustee of the John F. Kennedy Center for the Performing Arts, and was honorary consultant in American Letters at the Library of Congress. Ellison was married twice, but details of his first marriage are unavailable; in 1946 he married Fanny McConnell. Ralph Ellison died in New York City on April 16, 1994. ❖

Thematic and Structural Analysis

The title character of Ralph Ellison's *Invisible Man*, a novel about an unnamed young black man's political and racial self-discovery, admires Louis Armstrong's song "What Did I Do to Be So Black and Blue." In the **prologue** he asks the same question about his own life, wondering at his fate as a black man in an indifferent racist society. The novel itself is structured like a jazz performance; the narrator adopts a fluid, improvisational voice and introduces themes in the prologue that run, elaborated and varied, throughout his story.

The setting of the prologue is surreal: The narrator, who has rejected society after years of hope and political involvement, lives on the border of Harlem in an underground room brilliantly lit by 1,369 light bulbs. The heat and electricity are pirated from Monopolated Light & Power, which, because of the speaker's "invisibility," cannot detect the source of the power drain. There are subversive advantages, the narrator comically implies, to going unseen in society. This invisibility clearly symbolizes the racism indigenous to America in the first half of the century—the speaker says he is unseen not because he is a "spook" but because "people refuse to see me . . . they see only my surroundings, themselves, or figments of their imagination." The narrator's comedy quickly mixes with rage as he recalls the constant affronts his imperceptibility has engendered. In one instance, an accidental jostle and automatic slur spurred him to demand an apology from a white passerby. Receiving instead only confused epithets, he beat and kicked the man, preparing even to cut his throat before he realized that the victim regarded the assault as terrifyingly unmotivated, "a walking nightmare." Stunned by his own inefficacy, the narrator burst out laughing and ran from the scene.

These often grotesque strains of comedy and violence, as well as the motifs of sight and blindness, darkness and light, recur throughout the book. Added to these are the themes of hallucinogenics, drunkenness, nightmares, music, and oratory, the powers of which the narrator also explores in the prologue.

Smoking marijuana and listening to Louis Armstrong, he leads the reader into the cultural "depths" of the music, hearing below the fast tempo a slower black spiritual, the call and response of a black congregation's sermon, and the laughter and tears of a slave woman whose master has died. The prologue ends with a reaffirmation of the narrator's belief in action and a defense of his phantom attacks on society's "dreamers and sleepwalkers," who refuse to perceive him.

The narrator then begins to tell his life history, in some ways an extended series of initiations into various institutions, each ending in betrayal, explosive violence, nightmarish perceptual distortion, and a loss of control. The first of these experiences takes place in **chapter one**, when the narrator, the high school valedictorian, is asked to give his speech on black humility as the "very essence of progress" to a gathering of his town's leading white citizens. The other entertainments are to be a boxing match or "battle royal" among nine black roughs and, the boys learn on entering the ballroom, a striptease. The narrator reacts with horror as the moral leaders of the community, drunk, force the black boys to stand in front of a naked blond dancer as she tantalizes them with her movements. The tempo of the dance music quickens, the white men begin to touch and chase her, and she narrowly escapes, leaving the traumatized black youths to go through with the fight. The narrator is forced to participate, and all ten youths are blindfolded and egged on with racial slurs in a crazed battle, which ends with the narrator getting knocked out. They are then urged to collect their prize money from a pile of cash strewn on a rug, which turns out to be electrically wired. Scrambling for coins, shoved and pushed by the drunken audience, they are repeatedly shocked with intolerable volts of electricity. Only after this wild manhandling is the narrator asked to give his valedictory address. Showing him weak, bloodied, yelling, and choking over the noise of the audience, Ellison depicts his hero's speech on racial harmony with heavy irony.

The performance nonetheless earns him a scholarship to a prestigious southern black college, an idyllic bastion of learning where he hopes to follow in the footsteps of the distinguished black president, Dr. Bledsoe (**chapter two**). But the speaker's dreams are shattered in the spring of his junior year when, during Founder's Day, he gets the job of chauffeuring one of the college's wealthy white trustees. Mr. Norton asks the narrator to drive into the countryside during a break between meetings, meanwhile lecturing him on his luck at being part of a "great dream become reality." Instead of showing him the sanitized, idealized version of black life in the South that Dr. Bledsoe would like him to see, the protagonist unintentionally drives Mr. Norton through an impoverished black area, thus, in the words of Dr. Bledsoe, "dragg[ing] the entire race into the slime!" Mr. Norton, first unaware of his surroundings, continues with a story about his beautiful daughter, "too pure for life," to whose memory he has dedicated his philanthropy. The trustee then notices a rundown shack—a former slave cottage—belonging to Jim Trueblood, a delinquent black sharecropper, and orders the car to stop. Here Mr. Norton learns with horror of Trueblood's incestuous relationship with his daughter, who, along with her mother, is visibly pregnant. Mr. Norton listens to the farmer with a mixture of horror and fascination, hearing the man's story of poverty, lust, nightmares, and violence. The effect on the white man is catastrophic; he appears on the verge of a stroke and, pleading for whiskey, orders the narrator to drive on.

As in so many of the narrator's misadventures, his well-intentioned decision, in this case to take Mr. Norton to the closest bar, the Golden Day, only leads to greater calamity. The Golden Day is a brothel to which a group of mentally ill black war veterans is taken once a week. In **chapter three** they have already arrived when the narrator brings his half-conscious charge inside. With the ironic clairvoyance of the insane, they recognize Mr. Norton as a Thomas Jefferson, a John D. Rockefeller, and even the Messiah. A riot breaks out almost immediately. Their supervisor, a giant black man named Supercargo, calls for order, but the veterans charge him, knocking him down and beating him unconscious. The narrator rescues Mr. Norton by taking him upstairs. He is greeted by prostitutes and a deranged former doctor who, after reviving the trustee, describes his wrongful treatment as a member of the medical profession. The doctor accuses the hero of delusional submission to white society and laughs scornfully at Mr. Norton's patronage of the college, driving the two back downstairs. Mr. Norton narrowly escapes the riotous crowd below and returns to campus in a state of shock.

Dr. Bledsoe's wrath falls on the narrator with unanticipated fervor (**chapter four**). Bledsoe tells him that he should have manipulated Mr. Norton: "We take these white folks where we want them to go, we show them what we want them to see." In a gesture emblematic of this maxim, Bledsoe composes his rage-distorted face to address the white trustee with humility and concern. The narrator then attends the proceedings of Founder's Day with guilt-ridden veneration, anticipating his expulsion.

Ellison's imagery in **chapter five**, describing the gathering students with "limbs stiff and voices now silent, as though on exhibit even in the dark, and the moon a white man's blood-shot eye," is typically vivid and surreal. The students sing black spirituals for the benefit of the visiting white patrons, and then the Reverend Homer A. Barbee gives a speech remembering the college's original black founder. In one of the striking examples of oratory that fill Ellison's novel, he passionately invokes the messianic life of the Founder—born a slave. The narrator stumbles from the chapel, shamed beyond words for his betrayal of the college.

He then goes to Dr. Bledsoe, who reprimands him ferociously (**chapter six**). The college president describes the necessity of lying to whites ("[T]he only way to please a white man is to tell him a lie!") and talks about the black man's social invisibility ("You're nobody, son. You don't exist. . ."). He proclaims that he has created a place for himself in the country's all-white society by playing the role of the deferential black yea-sayer. The interview evokes memories of the dying words of the narrator's grandfather who, as Ellison describes in chapter one, led a life of exemplary humility and obedience but declared on his death bed that his acquiescence to whites was actually a subversive ploy to wrest control from them: "I want you to overcome 'em with yeses, undermine 'em with grins. . . let 'em swoller you till they vomit or burst open."

At Dr. Bledsoe's office, the speaker is shocked but relieved to hear that his punishment will be only to leave for the semester. He is sent to New York with Dr. Bledsoe's sealed letters of introduction and told to find work for the summer. On the bus to New York (**chapter seven**), the despondent narrator meets the doctor from the Golden Day again, who also advises him to drop his idealistic notions of race. "Play the game, but don't believe in it. . . ," he tells the hero. Yet the narrator arrives in New York filled with dreams of success. The bustle of the big city temporarily startles him—the intermingling of blacks and whites and the crush of the subway, where he is pushed against an indifferent fat white lady—but he makes his way eagerly to the Men's House in Harlem.

The narrator optimistically reports to various Wall Street offices with Dr. Bledsoe's personal letters but without success. Finally he delivers his last letter to an assistant of a Mr. Emerson (**chapter nine**). In a room draped with exotic tapestries, the dapper white man drops references to Freud and speaks enthusiastically of Harlem nightclubs. After reading the letter, he tries to dissuade the narrator from returning south. Finally he reveals that he is Mr. Emerson's son and shows the narrator Dr. Bledsoe's note, which vows permanent expulsion on the grounds that the narrator, who "has gone grievously astray," is a threat to the school. This betrayal shocks the narrator deeply.

He vows revenge on Dr. Bledsoe and applies for a job at a Long Island paint factory mentioned by Mr. Emerson (**chapter ten**). The narrator is hired because the company does not have to pay union wages to the "colored college boys" it employs. This segment contains some of the most explicit racial symbolism in the novel. Liberty Paints is famed for its "Optic White" paint color, "the purest white that can be found," which it supplies to the government. The paint can only be made by mixing ten drops of a secret formula into buckets of murky black paint. The narrator is set to this task, working frantically but accidentally ruining a batch by using the wrong formula. He is reprimanded and sent to assist Lucius Brockway, the engineer of paint production.

Deep in the basement among the rattling furnaces he meets this wiry old black man, who prefigures his own later underground self. Brockway is both paranoid and belligerent, convinced that the narrator has been sent as a spy. Tenaciously independent, he boasts that he alone knows the secrets of paint making, which the management has tried for years to acquire. He orders the narrator to watch several valve gauges and sets him to work shoveling coal.

During his lunch break, the narrator enters the locker room and discovers a union meeting in session. When the others learn that he works for Brockway, they turn against him, calling him a fink and voting to investigate him. The encounter makes him late for work. When Brockway hears his explanation, he attacks the protagonist in a rage, threatening to kill him, but the narrator eventually overpowers the older man, who breaks down and admits his deep hatred of unions. But at this point one of the valves begins to shriek. Brockway yells to the narrator to turn the white knob and then escapes, laughing, as the valve gives way and the hero is caught in an explosion of white paint. The painful loss of control and consciousness ("Somewhere an engine ground in furious futility, grating loudly until a pain shot around the curve of my head. . . ") recalls the end of the boxing match, when the narrator was brutally knocked out.

Chapter eleven recounts one of the most surreal episodes in the novel. The hero wakes up in a white room in the factory hospital. He is strapped to a machine and given electroshock therapy intended (as he overhears a doctor explain) to "produce the results of a prefrontal lobotomy . . . as complete a change of personality as you'll find in your famous fairy-tale cases of criminals transformed into amiable fellows." As his body shakes with the effects of the shocks, he hears one doctor remark, "They really do have rhythm, don't they?"

When the treatment ends, he finds that he can no longer remember his identity. A doctor tells him, "Well, boy, it looks as though you're cured. . . ." The narrator is released, sent to see the director, where he reacts with stabbing pain to the sound of his own name, which begins to trigger his memory. Told to seek work elsewhere, he stumbles back to Harlem, where a maternal woman, Miss Mary, takes pity on him and brings him to her home (**chapter twelve**). He moves into her boarding house and remains there for several peaceful months, unemployed and dependent on Mary's charity but quietly resistant to her lectures on leadership and responsibility.

One cold day he wanders the streets of Harlem and comes across an eviction (**chapter thirteen**). A crowd has gathered near a house where two white men are depositing an old black couple's belongings onto the street. Memories of his childhood return as he stares at the sad household clutter exposed to public scrutiny. When one of the men tries to block the old woman from reentering her home, the crowd threatens to grow violent. The narrator intervenes, calling the people to order with a rousing speech. Yet the man continues to refuse the woman entrance, and the crowd attacks him. The narrator then organizes the crowd to carry the furniture back inside. He controls the carnival atmosphere until the police arrive. Then, running to escape, he is approached by a short red-haired man who calls him "brother" and praises his speech. The man, Brother Jack, invites him to coffee and offers the wary hero a job in his organization. The narrator declines but reconsiders when he remembers his debts to Miss Mary.

In **chapter fourteen** the narrator is introduced to the Brotherhood, a secret quasi-Communist organization whose members meet at swank parties and talk elliptically of their mission to work "for a better world for all people." The narrator is stunned by the posh apartment to which he is taken and moved by Brother Jack's pronouncement of his future as the next Booker T. Washington. The Brotherhood offers him a large salary, provided he sever all ties with his past and adopt a new name and residence. During the ensuing cocktail party, one of the white brothers, thoroughly intoxicated, asks the narrator to sing a black spiritual. Others are embarrassed by his racist stereotyping, and the narrator downplays the offense. Nonetheless he goes home wondering how much he can trust his fellow brothers.

The narrator regretfully leaves Mary's boarding house to the banging of a broken furnace pipe, buying new clothes and moving to an apartment on the Upper East Side (**chapter fifteen**). That evening Brother Jack and a coterie of party members take him to give a speech at a rally in Harlem (**chapter sixteen**). After an initial hesitation, he forges a bond with the audience, rousing them to a fever pitch. The brothers are appalled, deeming the speech politically irresponsible. Because Brother Jack defends him, the narrator is allowed to keep his job on the condition that he go through three months of indoctrination into party principles under the guidance of Brother Hambro. He agrees, leaving the meeting convinced that he has finally found a way "to have a part in making the big decisions, of seeing through the mystery of how the country, the world, really operated."

The novel leaps over the narrator's tutoring to his first assignment as chief spokesman of the Harlem District (**chapter seventeen**). Brother Jack brings him to the district headquarters, where, at the committee meeting, he meets Brother Tod Clifton, a handsome, charismatic young black leader sporting a scar from a recent fight with a rival organization of black nationalists. The hero also meets the head of this organization, the radical black separatist Ras the Exhorter, when he and Clifton organize a street rally. Ras's henchmen break up the gathering, knocking out street lamps and beating men with lead pipes. The scene, pitting blacks against blacks, recalls the earlier battle royal. At one point Ras knocks Clifton down and threatens him with a knife, demanding his reason for staying with the interracial Brotherhood: "You my brother, mahn. Brothers are the same color. . . ." In an impassioned speech Ras emphasizes the need for black solidarity and repeatedly tries to convince Clifton, whom he calls a "black king," to join his party. The narrator breaks up the fight and ignores Ras's threats, but Clifton admits that he is troubled by the speech and wonders if "sometimes a man has to plunge outside history."

Nonetheless the narrator proves a successful organizer, and within weeks the Brotherhood clinches power in the district. The narrator's fame spreads rapidly; for a short stretch he lives "dominated by the all-embracing idea of Brotherhood." Then he receives an anonymous letter warning him of jealousy among the white leaders (**chapter eighteen**). Soon a white member, Brother Wrestrum, accuses the narrator of self-promotion. In a scene evoking the arbitrary vindictiveness of the union meeting, the members vote for an investigation and order the narrator temporarily demoted, sending him downtown to lecture on the "Woman Question."

In **chapter nineteen** the narrator gives his first speech on women's issues, and an eager female member of the audience invites him home to discuss the question further. In her elegant apartment, she aggressively seduces him. Afterward, he worries that the affair might have been a setup to orchestrate his downfall. But a more urgent problem intervenes: Brother Clifton disappears, and the narrator is asked to return to the rudderless Harlem District.

He finds that during his monthlong absence the Brotherhood has fallen into disrepute in Harlem (**chapter twenty**). Patrons confront him at the local bar, the district headquarters are deserted, and he is pointedly excluded from the central committee's meeting. Walking along Forty-third Street after enduring this latest affront, he stops to listen to a street vendor's spiel and recognizes Clifton selling "Sambo Boogie Woogie paper dolls." Before the narrator can confront him, Clifton disappears to avoid the police. The hero, amazed, wanders on and runs into the sideshow a second time. When a policeman barks at Clifton, his patience breaks, and he turns and knocks the officer down. As Clifton crouches to spring, the cop shoots him dead. After witnessing this horrific tableau, the narrator roams the streets bewildered by Clifton's desertion. He watches a group of apolitical zoot-suiters riding the subway back to Harlem and witnesses a petty shoplifting, wondering what real effect the Brotherhood has had on the black community.

Returning to his office, the narrator throws his energy into an open-air funeral for Clifton. The public showing is tremendous, yet when he stands to give the funeral address the narrator finds his political ideology falls flat. He makes a despondent, fatalistic pronouncement. He returns to his office to discover it full of grim-faced white party members, who call Clifton a traitor and accuse the narrator of playing up the race issue (**chapter twenty-two**). When the narrator insists that he was giving the people of Harlem the guidance and action they craved, Brother Jack answers, "We do not shape our policies to the mistaken and infantile notions of the man on the street. Our job is not to ask them what they think, but to *tell* them!" Brother Jack shocks the narrator by pulling out his own eye—it is artificial!—and dropping it in a glass of water. His real eye had been lost in the name of discipline, he says, admonishing the hero to obey with the same selflessness.

The brothers leave the protagonist to wander the darkened streets of Harlem, where he runs across Ras leading a rally (**chapter twenty-three**). The two argue about Clifton's death, and the narrator leaves to escape Ras's henchmen. He decides to disguise himself, but when he buys a pair of dark sunglasses and a wide-brimmed hat, he is immediately mistaken for someone named Rinehart. A heavily perfumed young woman tries to pick him up. Above the summer blare of cars and radios, he hears Ras continuing to incite the crowd. The black leader yells, "It is time Ras the Exhorter become Ras the DESTROYER!" and calls for action. In this mood of increasing tension, passersby continue to mistake the hero for Rinehart. He learns through his various encounters that the man is a womanizer, gambler, mob leader, and pimp. Then he stumbles into a church meeting and realizes that Rinehart is also a crooked minister, robbing his elderly congregation of their cash.

The narrator makes a last-ditch effort to restore his beliefs, visiting his former party tutor, Hambro, who tells him that the party's control of the Harlem District will have to be sacrificed for the greater good of the Brotherhood. Here he learns that "Rinehartism—cynicism" is not far from party policy: Hambro dismisses his charges of charlatanism with the argument that "it's impossible not to take advantage of the people." The narrator sees in the party's call for "scientific objectivity" the cruelty of the factory hospital's shock-therapy machine. He leaves angry and disillusioned, determined to imitate Rinehart and follow his grandfather's advice to gain control of the organization: "They were forcing me to Rinehart's methods, so bring on the scientists!"

He begins by downplaying his district's incidents of violence and falsifying a new list of members. The tactic seems to work, and he regains favor at the next meeting. He also hatches a plan to seduce an important member's wife to learn secret information. He finds a willing partner in a rich, lonely white woman named Sybil, married to one of the Brotherhood's "big shots," whom he invites to his apartment. Here he plies her with drinks and presses her for secrets. Unfortunately she has nothing to tell but, in an increasingly drunken fervor, urges him to enact a rape scene with her. The hero, both disgusted and amused, watches her drop off to sleep. They are roused by a phone call reporting riots in Harlem. Drunkenly stumbling into the night, the narrator tries to procure Sybil a taxi, while she begs to be taken along. He sends her downtown, but she reappears, running barefoot along 110th Street. He finds another cab, finally cajoling her to leave.

The narrator arrives in Harlem to find a nightmarish cityscape of shattered storefronts and surging bands of looters (**chapter twenty-five**). Alarms wail and gunshots ring out. He falls, nicked in the head by a bullet, but some men help him up, and he joins their band of looters, passing through streets of carnivalesque abandon. Their leader, Dupre, organizes the burning of a run-down tenement that his landlord has refused to fix. Amid various protests, he and his men torch the disease-ridden building.

The narrator runs on in the dark, stopping to help a man twist his own tourniquet and dodging police. He realizes that the Brotherhood must have planned the race riot, sacrificing Harlem for the sake of propaganda. His cynical acquiescence has not served as resistance to the Brotherhood, but rather as a tool, facilitating the party's plan. A final chilling image arrests his thoughts—seven naked white female mannequins hanging from a lamppost.

Then, as in a nightmare, he sees Ras the Destroyer dressed in the costume of an Abyssinian chieftain charging at him on horseback. The narrator protests that Ras, too, is being manipulated by the Brotherhood: "They deserted you so that in your despair you'd follow this man to your destruction." Ras throws a spear at the narrator, calling him a traitor and ordering him to be hanged. As he faces imminent death, the narrator realizes the absurdity of the causes he has supported and the hatred soon to bring about his death, as well as the truth about his own invisibility—he is just one small black man about to be extinguished by another. Empowered by the thought that it is "better to live out one's own absurdity than die for that of others," he throws Ras's spear, catching the chieftain in the jaw, and narrowly escapes through a looted store.

He tries to make his way downtown, stumbling with the blind disorientation experienced in so many of the novel's climaxes. A gang of hoodlums see him and give chase. While running, he falls through an open manhole into a coal cellar. When he refuses to give the gang his briefcase, they cover the hole, trapping him. He tries to burn a torch by lighting all of the important documents he has saved—his high school diploma, his Brotherhood papers, the paper doll from Brother Clifton—but cannot find a way out. Caught in a "state neither of dreaming nor of waking," he has a vision of disputing his former role models and disavowing his earlier illusions. He awakes to the realization that he cannot return to his former life.

Ellison's narration now returns to the fictional present, with a tentatively optimistic **epilogue**. Having made the cellar his home and having realized that the world outside is just as "concrete, ornery, vile and sublimely wonderful as before," the narrator finally tells us "that America is woven of many strands; I would recognize them and let it so remain. . . . Life is to be lived, not controlled; and humanity is won by continuing to play in the face of certain defeat." Despite the fact that he cannot be seen, he concludes that "there's a possibility that even an invisible man has a socially responsible role to play." In a decision that suggests Ellison's lingering hope for public action in race relations, the narrator ends by announcing his plan to break his hibernation. ✤

—*Anna Guillemin*
Princeton University

List of Characters

The *Invisible Man* is the rhetorically flamboyant unnamed narrator of Ellison's novel. He is invisible not because he is a "spook" —literally unseen—but because he is a black man living in the racist atmosphere of America in the 1920s and '30s, unrecognized because of his skin color. The narrator's insistent, cadenced oratorical style sweeps the reader into his world as he looks back, from the seclusion of an underground coal cellar on the border of Harlem, on the past twenty years of his life. The narrator is an angry, embittered speaker who recalls, often with heavy sarcasm, his younger naive and hopeful self, both as a student at a black southern college and later as the Harlem District leader of a quasi-Communist movement in New York City. Like a classic picaresque hero, he falls unwittingly into a series of grotesque tragic-comic adventures that, with explosive violence, shatter his beliefs about race relations, the world, and his place in it.

Dr. Bledsoe is the president of the narrator's southern black college, an impressive paternal role model who nonetheless betrays the hero and expels him from the idyllic campus. His is a classic success story: He has risen from an illiterate boy to an influential spokesman for the race; he is a gracious, humble intermediary between the college and the white board of trustees; and he is the owner of two Cadillacs. When the narrator antagonizes one of the trustee members, he incurs the wrath of Dr. Bledsoe, who reveals both his true beliefs—"the only way to please a white man is to tell him a lie"—and the autocratic power with which he runs this seeming bastion of racial harmony.

Mr. Norton is the white northern college trustee whom the narrator unintentionally chauffeurs through a series of nightmarish incidents. In the process of meeting a black sharecropper, who has impregnated his own daughter, and witnessing a riot in a black bar and brothel, Mr. Norton is stripped of his illusions about the peaceful advancement of black society. He returns to the campus in shock.

Mr. Emerson, the son of one of the college trustees, interviews the narrator for a job and ends up showing him Dr. Bledsoe's damning sealed letter of introduction. He is a wealthy white patron of black art, who takes pity on this victim of Bledsoe's rage and tips him off to a job at the Liberty paint factory.

Mary is the motherly head of a boarding house in Harlem who takes in the narrator after his electroshock therapy at the paint factory's hospital. She offers him support during his months of unemployment, confident that he will eventually assist in the betterment of his race.

Brother Jack is one of the leaders of the clandestine "Brotherhood" in New York, a political movement that advocates the mobilization of the masses and scientific objectivity and that is clearly modeled on contemporary Communism. A sprightly red-haired man with a penetrating gaze, he selects the narrator as the new district leader for Harlem after seeing him lead a protest against an eviction. Brother Jack moves mysteriously between the swank parties of wealthy donors and the mass demonstrations of the underprivileged. He first defends the narrator against jealous party members but later sacrifices the Harlem District in a calculated play for propaganda.

Tod Clifton is another Brotherhood Harlem District leader, a strikingly handsome daredevil who fights with members from a rival movement and helps the narrator mobilize the community. His commitment to the Brotherhood is not absolute—he talks of the temptation to renounce ideology and "plunge out of history"—and when the narrator temporarily leaves Harlem, he disappears. The hero spots him several days later, selling demeaning black puppets on a street corner. When harassed by a policeman, Clifton resists and is shot. Clifton's funeral marks the narrator's real break from the Brotherhood: In the face of blatant racial violence he cannot bring himself to preach the objective ideological party line.

Ras the Exhorter is the narrator's political rival, the leader of a Harlem black separatist movement whose ornery henchmen regularly disrupt Brotherhood demonstrations. Based on the historical figure of Marcus Garvey, Ras represents the alternative to the narrator's political ideology: rejection both of whites and the principles of universal equality. When a race riot erupts in Harlem, Ras relishes the violence: Dressed in African garb, he charges through the streets on horseback and hurls spears at the police and the narrator.

Rinehart is an elusive resident of Harlem who represents another alternative to the narrator's Brotherhood. The narrator first learns of him when, disguised in sunglasses and the wide-brimmed hat of a zoot-suiter, he is mistaken by several beautiful women for their protector. Rinehart is the ultimate con man, a corrupt minister, a gambler, and a pimp. The narrator briefly decides to imitate him, selfishly abusing his power to get back at the Brotherhood.

Sybil is the pampered wife of a white party leader whom the narrator, disillusioned by Clifton's death, uses for political purposes. She eagerly accepts his invitation home and, in the drunken flirtation that follows, reveals her ignorance of her husband's position and her predilection for interracial rape fantasies, casting the narrator as "Brother Taboo-with-whom-all-things-are-possible." She last appears on 110th Street, demanding to be taken to Harlem as the narrator loads her into a cab headed downtown. ❖

Critical Views

[Saul Bellow (b. 1915) is one of the most distinguished American novelists of the century and the author of such acclaimed works as *The Adventures of Augie March* (1953), *Herzog* (1964), and *Humboldt's Gift* (1975). In this review of *Invisible Man,* Bellow champions the novel by claiming that it transcends issues of race and becomes a universal work about humanity.]

I was keenly aware, as I read this book ⟨*Invisible Man*⟩, of a very significant kind of independence in the writing. For there is a "way" for Negro novelists to go at their problems, just as there are Jewish or Italian "ways." Mr. Ellison has not adopted a minority tone. If he had done so, he would have failed to establish a true middle-of-consciousness for everyone.

Negro Harlem is at once primitive and sophisticated; it exhibits the extremes of instinct and civilization as few other American communities do. If a writer dwells on the peculiarity of this, he ends with an exotic effect. And Mr. Ellison is not exotic. For him this balance of instinct and culture or civilization is not a Harlem matter; it is *the* matter, German, French, Russian, American, universal, a matter very little understood. It is thought that Negroes and other minority people, kept under in the great status battle, are in the instinct cellar of dark enjoyment. This imagined enjoyment provokes envious rage and murder; and then it is a large portion of human nature itself which becomes the fugitive murderously pursued. In our society Man—Himself—is idolized and publicly worshipped, but the single individual must hide himself underground and try to save his desires, his thoughts, his soul, his invisibility. He must return to himself, learning self-acceptance and rejecting all that threatens to deprive him of his manhood.

This is what I make of *Invisible Man*. It is not by any means faultless; I don't think the hero's experiences in the Communist party are as original in conception as other parts of the book, and his love affair with a white woman is all too brief, but it is an immensely moving novel and it has greatness.

—Saul Bellow, "Man Underground," *Commentary* 13, No. 6 (June 1952): 609

ROBERT BONE ON RALPH ELLISON AND LITERARY TRADITIONS

[Robert Bone (b. 1924), formerly the chairman of the department of English at Columbia University Teachers College, is the author of *Down Home: Origins of the Afro-American Short Story* (1975) and the celebrated treatise *The Negro Novel in America* (1958), from which the following extract is taken. Here, Bone explores the authors and literary movements that influenced Ellison in the writing of *Invisible Man*.]

In repudiating naturalism, Ellison turns to the broad tradition established by Joyce, Kafka, and Faulkner. Like them, he finds the shattered forms of postimpressionism most effective in portraying the chaos of the modern world. But Ellison apprehends this chaos through a particular cultural screen. It is precisely his vision of the possibilities of Negro life that has burst the bonds of the naturalistic novel. His style, like that of any good writer, flows from his view of reality, but this in turn flows from his experience as a Negro. His unique experience, Ellison insists, requires unique literary forms, and these he tries to provide from the raw material of Negro culture. It is a major contribution to the evolution of the Negro novel.

What stylistic resources can a folk culture offer the creative writer? To begin with, there is the rhetorical skill of the American Negro, whose verbal expression, under slavery, was necessarily oral. The revival meeting, the funeral sermon, the graduation address, the political speech are used to good account in *Invisible Man*. Then there are the sonorous biblical phrases which season the dialogue, along with the spicier ingredients of jive. To freshen up a jaded diction, a whole new vocabulary is available—terms evocative of the numbers racket, of voodoo charms, of racing sheets, of spiritualist cure-alls, of the jazz world, the boxing ring, the ball park, the bar-room—in a word, of Harlem.

One of the nuances of Negro speech exploited by Ellison is the sheer delight in the verbal play, in pure *sound,* which might be experienced by a child—or a transplanted people—in learning a new language. This is more readily sampled than described: "Then came the squad of drum majorettes . . . who pranced and twirled and just plain girled in the enthusiastic interest of Brotherhood." Closer to folk origin is this bit of dialogue: "I'll verse you but I won't curse you—My name is Peter Wheatstraw, I'm the Devil's only son-in-law, so roll 'em! You a southern boy ain't you?" Intellectualized once more: a college professor, lecturing on Joyce, remarks, "Stephen's problem, like ours, was not actually one of creating the uncreated conscience of his race, but of creating the uncreated features of his face."

In their spoken idiom a people may unwittingly betray their innermost thoughts and feelings. The things that they laugh at are equally revealing of their deepest values, and Ellison's treatment of in-group humor is masterful. He displays a true comic genius, ranging from his sly description of a belligerent colored bartender ("He sliced the white heads off of a couple of beers with an ivory paddle") to the raucous comedy of the riot scene (in which one looter asks indignantly, "With all them hats in there and I'm going to come out with anything but a *Dobbs?*"). With his heritage of laughter-to-keep-from-crying, Ellison balances adroitly on the thin line which divides comedy from tragedy, and this double vision, this ability to perceive events as at once poignant and faintly ridiculous, introduces a subtle emotional tension into the novel. The solvent for this tension is a pervasive irony, through which the author achieves a satisfactory distance from his experience.

Jazz and the blues form an important part of Ellison's consciousness (he has played jazz trumpet since high school) and consequently of his style. The tone of the novel, for example, is established in the prologue by Louis Armstrong's not-so-innocent question,

What did I do
To be so black
And blue?

The blue note is sustained by occasional snatches of blues lyrics, and by such passages as this: "I strode along, hearing the cartman's song become a lonesome, broad-toned whistle now that flowered at the end of each phrase into a tremulous, blue-toned chord. And in its flutter and swoop I heard the sound of a railroad train highballing it, lonely across the lonely night."

Jazz forms have also influenced what might be called the composition of the novel. Something is always going on in the background of Ellison's prose—something not quite heard at first, but nevertheless insistent, which produces a feeling of depth and resonance when finally perceived. The circling, diving, plummeting pigeons which hover in the background during the shooting of Tod Clifton will serve to illustrate the point. It is a passage thoroughly characteristic of Ellison's technique: he writes a "melody" (thematic line) and then orchestrates it.

Not to overstate the case for a distinctive Negro style, some general literary influences should be acknowledged. At farthest remove is Flaubert, to whom can be traced a tightness of style in which no detail is superfluous, no word or phrase without its place in the design. In sifting through his American tradition for evidence of a usable past, Ellison discovered our classical novelists of the 19th century, and especially Melville and Twain. In them, he notes, he found a greater sense of responsibility for the future of democracy than among his own contemporaries. But above all, he found a sense of the unknown and mysterious frontiers of American life which corresponded to his experience as a Negro. "In their imaginative economy," he writes, "the Negro symbolized both the man lowest down and the mysterious, underground aspect of human personality."

Closer at hand is his debt to Faulkner and Eliot. To the extent that Ellison's style is directly imitative, it is Faulknerian. The lengthy sentences, the rapid flow of consciousness conveyed by a string of participles, the series of abstract nouns joined together by an overworked conjunction—these are familiar trademarks. From Faulkner, too, comes a sense of the grotesque, the monstrous, the outrageous in Southern life. The incest scene in *Invisible Man*, for example, is unimaginable without the precedent of Popeye. On the whole, it is more the symbolist of *The Sound and the Fury* than the local colorist of *The Hamlet* to whom Ellison pays the supreme compliment, but both elements are present in his style to a degree.

There are direct echoes of Eliot, too, in *Invisible Man*, and one of the epigraphs (the other is from Melville's *Benito Cereno*) is from *Family Reunion*. But Ellison's real debt stems from Eliot's insistence upon the importance of tradition. It was this reassurance from a major contemporary that fortified him in his determination to anchor his fiction firmly in his Negro heritage. It was Eliot who taught him to value a past which was both painful and precious and, flinching neither from slavery nor incest nor prostitution nor chaos itself, to assimilate even his negative heritage, conquering it, transforming it into an asset, a weapon.

—Robert Bone, *The Negro Novel in America* (New Haven: Yale University Press, 1958), pp. 198–201

EARL H. ROVIT ON *INVISIBLE MAN* AS A COMIC NOVEL

[Earl H. Rovit (b. 1927) is a former professor of English at City College of the City University of New York. He has written studies of Elizabeth Madox Roberts (1960) and Ernest Hemingway (1963) as well as several novels. In this extract, Rovit sees *Invisible Man* as a deeply comic work that uses humor to underscore its moral focus.]

The most obvious comment one can make about Ralph Ellison's *Invisible Man* is that it is a profoundly comic work. But the obvious is not necessarily either simple or self-explanatory, and it seems to me that the comic implications of Ellison's novel are elusive and provocative enough to warrant careful examination both in relation to the total effect of the novel itself and the American cultural pattern from which it derives. ⟨. . .⟩

First it should be noted that Ellison's commitment to what Henry James has termed "the American joke" has been thoroughly deliberated and undisguised. Ellison once described penetratingly the ambiguous *locus* of conflicting forces within which the American artist has had always to work: "For the ex-colonials, the declaration of an American identity meant the assumption of a mask, and it imposed not only the discipline of national self-consciousness, it gave Americans an ironic awareness of the joke that always lies between appearance and reality, between the discontinuity of social tradition and that sense of the past which clings to the mind. And perhaps even an awareness of the joke that society is man's creation, not God's." This kind of ironic awareness may contain bitterness and may even become susceptible to the heavy shadow of despair, but the art which it produces has been ultimately comic. It will inevitably probe the masks of identity and value searching relentlessly for some deeper buried reality, but it will do this while accepting the fundamental necessity for masks and the impossibility of ever discovering an essential face beneath a mask. That is to say, this comic stance will accept with the same triumphant gesture both the basic absurdity of all attempts to impose meaning on the chaos of life, and the necessary converse of this, the ultimate significance of absurdity itself.

Ellison's *Invisible Man* is comic in this sense almost in spite of its overtly satirical interests and its excursions into the broadly farcical. Humorous as many of its episodes are in themselves—the surreal hysteria of the scene at the Golden Day, the hero's employment at the Liberty Paint Company, or the expert dissection of political entanglements in Harlem—these are the materials which clothe Ellison's joke and which, in turn, suggest the shape by which the joke can be comprehended. The pith of Ellison's comedy reverberates on a level much deeper than these incidents, and as in all true humor, the joke affirms and denies simultaneously—accepts and rejects with the same uncompromising passion, leaving not a self-cancelling neutralization of momentum, but a sphere of moral conquest, a humanized cone of light at the very heart of darkness. *Invisible Man,* as Ellison has needlessly insisted in rebuttal to those critics who would treat the novel as fictionalized sociology or as a dramatization of archetypal images, is an artist's attempt to create a *form*. And fortunately Ellison has been quite explicit in describing what he means by *form;* in specific reference to the improvisation of the jazz-musician he suggests that form represents "a definition of his identity: as an individual, as a member of the collectivity, and as a link in the chain of tradition." But note that each of these definitions of identity must be individually exclusive and mutually contradictory on any logical terms. Because of its very pursuit after the uniqueness of individuality, the successful definition of an individual must define out the possibilities of generalization into "collectivity" or "tradition." But herein for Ellison in his embrace of a notion of fluid amorphous identity lies the real morality and humor in mankind's art and men's lives—neither of which have much respect for the laws of formal logic.

—Earl H. Rovit, "Ralph Ellison and the American Comic Tradition," *Wisconsin Studies in Contemporary Literature* 1, No. 3 (Fall 1960): 34–35

JONATHAN BAUMBACH ON GOTHIC ELEMENTS IN *INVISIBLE MAN*

[Jonathan Baumbach (b. 1933), a professor of English at Brooklyn College of the City University of New York, is a novelist, short story writer, and critic. In this extract from an article on Ellison included in his collection of essays, *The Landscape of Nightmare* (1965), Baumbach argues that, in spite of its obvious concern with issues of race and society, *Invisible Man* is a modern Gothic novel.]

Despite its obvious social implications, Ellison's novel is a modern gothic, a Candide-like picaresque set in a dimly familiar nightmare landscape called the United States. Like *The Catcher in the Rye, A Member of the Wedding,* and *The Adventures of Augie March,* Ellison's novel chronicles a series of initiatory experiences through which its naïve hero learns, to his disillusion and horror, the way of the world. However, unlike these other novels of passage, *Invisible Man* takes place, for the most part, in the uncharted spaces between the conscious and the unconscious, in the semilit darkness where nightmare verges on reality and the external world has all the aspects of a disturbing dream. Refracted by satire, at times, cartooned, Ellison's world is at once surreal and real, comic and tragic, grotesque and normal—our world viewed in its essentials rather than its externals.

The Negro's life in our white land and time is, as Ellison knows it, a relentless unreality, unreal in that the Negro as a group is loved, hated, persecuted, feared, and envied, while as an individual he is unfelt, unheard, unseen—to all intents and purposes invisible. The narrator, who is also the novel's central participant, never identifies himself by name. Though he experiences several changes of identity in the course of the novel, Ellison's hero exists to the reader as a man without an identity, an invisible "I." In taking on a succession of identities, the invisible hero undergoes an increasingly intense succession of disillusioning experiences, each one paralleling and anticipating the one following it. The hero's final loss of illusion forces him underground into the coffin (and womb) of the earth to be either finally buried or finally reborn.

The narrator's grandfather, whom he resembles (identity is one of the major concerns of the novel), is the first to define the terms of existence for him. An apparently meek man all his life, on his deathbed the grandfather reveals:

> "Son, after I'm gone I want you to keep up the good fight. I never told you, but our life is a war and I have been a traitor all my born days, a spy in the enemy's country ever since I give up my gun back in the Reconstruction. Live with your head in the lion's mouth. I want you to overcome 'em with yesses, undermine 'em with grins, agree 'em to death and destruction, let 'em swoller you till they vomit or bust wide open."

Though at the time he understands his grandfather's ambiguous creed only imperfectly, the hero recognizes that it is somehow his heritage. In a sense, the old man's code of acquiescent resistance is an involved justification of his nonresistance; it is a parody on itself, yet the possibility always remains that it is, in some profound, mysterious way, a meaningful ethic. On a succession of occasions, the hero applies his grandfather's advice, "agreeing 'em to death," in order to understand its import through discovering its efficacy. On each occasion, however, it is he, not " 'em," who is victimized. Consequently, the hero suffers a sense of guilt—not for having compromised himself but for failing somehow to effect his grandfather's ends. Ironically, he also feels guilty for deceiving the white "enemy," though he has "agreed them" not to death or destruction, only to renewed complacency. For example:

> When I was praised for my conduct I felt a guilt that in some way I was doing something that was really against the wishes of the white folks, that if they had understood they would have desired me to act just the opposite, that I should have been sulky and mean, and that really would have been what they wanted, even though they were fooled and thought they wanted ed me to act as I did.

The hero's cynical obsequiousness has self-destructive consequences. Having delivered a high school graduation speech advocating humility as the essence of progress, he is invited to deliver his agreeable oration to a meeting of the town's leading white citizens. Before he is allowed to speak, however, he is subjected to a series of brutal degradations, which teach him, in effect, the horror of the humility he advocates. In this episode, the first of his initiatory experiences, the invisible man's role is symbolically prophesied. The hero, along with nine other Negro boys, is put into a prize ring, then is blindfolded and coerced into battling his compatriots. Duped by the whites, the Negro unwittingly fights himself; his potency, which the white man envies and fears, is mocked and turned against him to satisfy the brutal whims of his persecutor. That the bout is preceded by a nude, blond belly dancer whom the boys are forced to watch suggests the prurience underlying the victimizer's treatment of his victim. The degrading prizefight, a demonstration of potency to titillate the impotent, in which the Negro boys blindly flail one another to entertain the sexually aroused stag audience, parallels the riot in Harlem at the end of the novel, which is induced by another institution of white civilization, the Brotherhood (a fictional guise for the Communist party). Once again Negro fights against Negro (Ras the Destroyer against the hero), although this time it is for the sake of "Brotherhood," a euphemism for the same inhumanity. In both cases, the Negro unwittingly performs the obscene demands of his enemy. In magnification, Harlem is the prize

ring where the Negroes, blindfolded this time by demagoguery, flail at each other with misdirected violence. The context has changed from South to North, from white citizens to
the Brotherhood, from a hired ballroom to all of Harlem, but
the implication remains the same: the Negro is victimized by
having his potency turned against himself by his impotent persecutor.

> —Jonathan Baumbach, "Nightmare of a Native Son: *Invisible*
> *Man* by Ralph Ellison" (1963), *The Landscape of Nightmare:*
> *Studies in the Contemporary American Novel* (New York: New
> York University Press, 1965), pp. 68–71

EDWARD MARGOLIES ON BLACK NATIONALISM IN *INVISIBLE*
MAN

[Edward Margolies (b. 1925) is a professor of English
and American studies at the College of Staten Island of
the City University of New York. He has written *The Art
of Richard Wright* (1969) and *Which Way Did He Go?
The Private Eye in Dashiell Hammett, Raymond
Chandler, Chester Himes, and Ross Macdonald* (1982).
In this extract from *Native Sons* (1968), Margolies
investigates the function and influence of black nationalism in Ellison's novel.]

⟨. . .⟩ if urban life awakens the hero to emotions of a specific
Negro historical identity, as opposed to what Ellison once
described as Southern rural "pre-individualistic attitudes" (that
is, an almost total absence of selfhood, a passive attitude
toward oneself as being part of an amorphous black mass), the
Depression expands these feelings to include an active sense of
social responsibility the hero now shares with many other city
Negroes. And the latter part of the novel deals with some of
the forces that endeavored to make political use of the new
awakening in Negro communities.

Black nationalism, the first of these, is represented in the figure of Ras the Exhorter, an exotic West Indian extremist. The

hero sees Ras violently addressing a street corner gathering when he first arrives in Harlem from the South. He pays little attention at the time but when he later involves himself with the Brotherhood (the Communist Party), Ras and his followers play a distinct role in his experiences. Ras, who suggests something of the colorful Marcus Garvey, preaches a doctrine of complete black virtue coupled with an utter distrust of the white man. Attired in Ethiopian garb, Ras makes a ludicrous figure, but his eloquence and passion more than make up for his lack of "program." As one of the hero's companions later puts it, Ras works on the "inside"; that is, he articulates the frustration, suspicion and anger the Negro has suppressed about his American experience.

The hero is recruited by the Brotherhood when, after witnessing the physical eviction of an elderly Negro couple from their tenement, he delivers a fiery speech protesting the injustice of it all to a gathering street crowd. Even here, Ellison suggests the specific Negro history that has ultimately placed the unhappy pair on the dreary Harlem sidewalk. He cites the pathetic paucity of personal effects they are allowed to keep, among them a small Ethiopian flag, a tintype of Abraham Lincoln, a manumission paper dated 1859, a pair of "knocking bones" used in minstrel shows, some faded and void insurance policies, and a "yellowing newspaper portrait of a huge black man with the caption: 'MARCUS GARVEY DEPORTED.'" The hero's passionate outburst evokes a small riot, whereupon the white evicters are pummeled and the Negro couple are triumphantly returned to their flat. The hero manages to escape before the police arrive, but his performance has meanwhile attracted the attention of one of the Brotherhood members, who pursues him and asks him to join the organization. His function, it appears, will be to address Negro gatherings on behalf of Brotherhood principles. He would, of course, have to learn what these are—and, after some reluctance, the hero agrees to do so.

Ellison perhaps devotes too much space proportionally to the Communist wooing of the Negro, but these are experiences he knew, after all, firsthand, and the Marxist emphasis on Negro history as being part of a larger dialectical process must have appealed to Ellison's ingrained aesthetic sense. In any event, his hero's Communist experiences are too complicated to chronicle fully. He becomes an authentic Harlem "spokesman," but even when he is most blinded by his Marxist rhetoric, there persist in the marrow of his being some suspicions regarding the relevance of his Negro experience to the notions of history he publicly upholds. Indeed, Ras's violent and chauvinistic opposition to Brotherhood ideals is closer to what he knows to be true. What he finally learns in the course of his radical adventures is that even for the Brothers, the Negro is a thing, an object, an instrument of power politics and of preordained historical design, rather than a divinely complex and complicated human mystery. He concludes, therefore, that he has been as invisible to the Brotherhood as he has been to all the others, and that the Brothers require his invisibility in order to delude themselves concerning their own historical identity. The white Brotherhood chieftain, Brother Jack, wears a glass eye, implying, of course, that he perceives only mechanistic history ("necessity") and not the accidental nature of human beings.

Yet his experiences as a radical are not a total loss. For one thing, the hero, like his author, has acquired an education of sorts regarding the Negro's role in history. If what the hero learns is at considerable variances from what the Brotherhood wanted him to learn, he does nonetheless take away with himself an added sense of his own importance. Second, and possibly more important, is that in making him a Harlem leader, the Brotherhood has unwittingly given him access to his fellow Negroes on a level he had hitherto seldom achieved. He discovers to his astonishment (and to the chagrin of the Brothers) a bond of love and shared experience that the outside world can never know.

—Edward Margolies, "History as Blues: Ralph Ellison's *Invisible Man*," *Native Sons: A Critical Study of Twentieth-Century Black American Authors* (Philadelphia: Lippincott, 1968), pp. 140–43

TONY TANNER ON THE POWERLESSNESS OF THE INVISIBLE
MAN

[Tony Tanner (b. 1935) is the director of English studies
at King's College, Cambridge. He has written many
critical studies, including *The Reign of Wonder: Naivety
and Reality in American Literature* (1965) and *Henry
James: The Writer and His Works* (1985). In this extract,
Tanner explores the reaction of the narrator of *Invisible
Man* to the mechanization of the modern world and
the various forces that seek to control his life.]

The point about all the representatives of social power that the
narrator encounters—teacher, preacher, doctor, factory-owner,
Party member, whatever—is that they all seek to control reality
and they believe that they can run it according to their plan. To
this extent one can say that they have a mechanizing attitude
towards reality, and it is no accident that the narrator is con-
stantly getting involved with literal machines (in the factory,
the hospital, etc.) as well as with what one might call the
mechanizers of consciousness, the servants of church, college
or Party. On the other hand there is the point that these institutions, these people at the social controls, do seem to give the
individual a role, a place in the scheme of things. At one stage
the narrator is enthusiastic about the Party, because it gives the
world a meaningful shape and himself an important role in it:
'everything could be controlled by our science. Life was all pattern and discipline.'

The alternative to the servile docility and rigid regulations of
the state college would seem to be the utter chaos of The
Golden Day Saloon, which with its fighting and drinking and
debauchery seems to be in continuous rehearsal for 'the end of
the world', as one mad participant proclaims it (see R. W. B.
Lewis's fine essay 'Days of Wrath and Laughter' for a discussion
of the apocalyptic hints in the novel). It may be more real,
more authentic than fabricated performances in the chapel at
the college, but in its utterly shapeless confusion it offers no
opportunities for self-development or self-discovery. Society
does indeed impose false surfaces on things; a point well made
at the paint factory where the narrator has to mix in a black

constituent which nevertheless produces a dazzling Optic White paint used for government buildings. It reminds the narrator of the white painted buildings of the campus; it also reminds him that The Golden Day had once been painted white but that now it was all flaking away. The fact that the paint is called Liberty Paint in conjunction with the suggestion that it is at least in part an optical illusion (the narrator can see a grey in the white which his overseer ignores or cannot detect) is a fairly clear irony; we are in fact 'caught' in the official version of reality—the painted surfaces—maintained by the constituted authorities. On the other hand, if you strip all the false paint away you are likely to be confronted with the merely chaotic 'truth' of The Golden Day. In the same way, the mechanizers and controllers of reality turn people into automata and manipulable dummies; but can a man achieve any visible shape or role if he refuses to join any of the existing patterns?

This is indeed the narrator's problem. When he is about to be sent away from the college he feels that he is losing the only identity that he has ever known. At this stage he equates a stable niche in the social structure with an identity, and for a long time his quest is for some defining and recognized employment. The matter of the letters from Bledsoe is instructive; they are supposed to be helping him find a job which might enable him to return to his higher education, whereas in fact they are treacherously advancing Bledsoe's scheme of keeping him as far away from college as possible. He feels all along that he is playing a part in some incomprehensible 'scheme', but it is only when the younger Emerson shows him one of the letters that he begins to understand. 'Everyone seemed to have some plan for me, and beneath that some more secret plan.' It is an essential part of his education that he should come to realize that 'everybody wanted to use you for some purpose' and that the way they recognize you, on and in their own terms, is not to be confused with your identity.

After his accident in the factory he undergoes what is in effect a process of rebirth—not organically but electrically. From his fall into the lake of heavy water and on to his coming to consciousness with a completely blank mind in a small glass-and-nickel box, and his subsequent struggle to get out, it reads like a mechanized parody of the birth process. The electrical treatment has temporarily erased his earlier consciousness and he cannot say who he is or what his name is. His only concern is to get out of the machine without electrocuting himself. 'I wanted freedom, not destruction . . . I could no more escape than I could think of my identity. Perhaps, I thought, the two things are involved with each other. When I discover who I am, I'll be free.' This, coming nearly halfway through the book, is a crucial turning-point. The machine is every system by which other people want to manipulate him and regulate his actions. In much the same way the Party gives him a new identity and tries to reprogramme him for its ends. The narrator is not a nihilist—he does not wish to smash the machine, knowing that he will probably be destroyed with it—but he wants to find some sort of freedom from the interlocking systems which make up society, and he realizes that it will have to be mainly an inner freedom. At the end he can look back and see that the individuals from various professions or parties who had sought to direct and use him 'were very much the same, each attempting to force his picture of reality upon me and neither giving a hoot in hell for how things looked to me.' This is why he wants to be free of all parties, all partial pictures, all the imposed and imprisoning constructs of society. This urge will bring him to a second rebirth near the end—this time a private, self-managed one. But before coming to that we should consider some of the advice and examples he has received from figures who are not on the side of the system-makers, not enlisted among the controllers.

His grandfather on his deathbed has given the advice to 'overcome 'em with yeses', and only by the end can the narrator see a possible hidden meaning in this exhortation. Before he leaves for New York, the vet in The Golden Day advises him that, once there, he should play the game without believing it: he explains that he will be 'hidden right out in the open' because 'they' will not expect him to know anything and therefore will not be able to see him. When asked by the narrator who 'they' refers to, he answers, 'Why the same *they* we always mean, the white folks, authority, the gods, fate, circumstances—the force that pulls your strings until you refuse to be pulled any more.' Three further things he says to the narrator are of particular importance. He tells him that much of his freedom will have to be 'symbolic'—a deeper truth perhaps than he knows for the boy who will ultimately find his freedom in the symbols called words. He says, 'Be your own father, young man,' an Oedipal echo (picking up the description we have already had of the narrator standing where three roads converge) and a warning to the boy that he will have to create an identity, not rely on assuming one already waiting for him. Thirdly, he bids him remember that the world is 'possibility'. And this anticipates the narrator's encounter with Rinehart which is perhaps the most important 'epiphany' in the book.

—Tony Tanner, *City of Words: American Fiction 1950–1970* (New York: Harper & Row, 1971), pp. 53–55

JERRY WASSERMAN ON THE STRUCTURE OF *INVISIBLE MAN*

[Jerry Wasserman (b. 1945), a professor of English at the University of British Columbia, is the editor of *Modern Canadian Plays* (1985). In this extract, Wasserman analyzes the structure of *Invisible Man* and some of Ellison's narrative techniques.]

The structure of *Invisible Man* consists of a series of false or superficial identities which the protagonist allows to be imposed upon him, and which he must finally discard in favor of his one true identity, his invisibility. His recognition and embrace of this identity closely resembles Bigger's. Initially, his self-acceptance is only partial; he too thinks he can profit from a public mask and soon finds the duality self-defeating. Like Bigger, the Invisible Man moves to a full and absolute choice of his newly-discovered self and finds freedom and a sense of wholeness. From there, however, he recognizes the need to move forward, like Genet's Blacks, to a new and more positive identity, to emerge from underground and transcend his invisibility.

As a young boy, even in the face of the white community's brutal racism, he can visualize himself as a potential Booker T.

Washington. But the security of his identity is disturbed by a number of men who have had to confront and reconcile their blackness and their social roles. The first is his grandfather, whose dying words are to haunt him all his life: "Our life is a war and I have been a traitor all my born days. . . . I want you to overcome 'em with yeses, undermine 'em with grins, agree 'em to death and destruction, let 'em swoller you till they vomit or bust wide open." Dr. Bledsoe is the earliest example in the boy's experience of the identity his grandfather seemed to advocate. With shock and despair the boy finds his model of a successful Negro to be a cynical opportunist behind the humble public persona. And it is from Bledsoe that he gets his first object-lesson in the politics of betrayal.

On his way to New York the boy meets another advocate of similar behavior, the "mad" vet. His advice, like Bledsoe's, is "play the game, but don't believe in it." He can do this, the vet tells him, because he is in effect invisible to whites. But neither his advice nor Bledsoe's nor the grandfather's ultimately proves as valuable as the example of the incestuous sharecropper, Jim Trueblood. He recounts to the boy how, struggling to learn to live with himself and the public shame of fathering his daughter's child, "I sings me some blues that night ain't never been sung before . . . and I makes up my mind that I ain't nobody but myself." Although at the time the boy gives no indication of understanding this total acceptance of self, it is essentially the manner in which he will finally come to terms with his own identity.

In New York his identity is completely stripped away. At the Liberty Paint plant, he resolves never again to "accept the foolishness of such old men" as his Bledsoe-like foreman, and thus cuts himself off from the past and the boy he has been. His surrealistic "lobotomy" completes the break with his former identity. When he regains consciousness he can no longer remember his name, and the question of his identity becomes an obsession. He is imprisoned in the machine—the white world—because he does not know who he is: "When I discover who I am, I'll be free."

His discovery begins in the cold winter streets of Harlem where he eats some hot yams. This act of what he calls "field niggerism" confirms his new freedom and total denial of his old self. "I am what I am," he proudly says, rejecting the artificial restrictions of his past. When asked to identify himself at the eviction, he answers, "I am who I am." And his ensuing speech, in which he becomes aware of himself as a member of an oppressed community, marks the real beginning of his self-creation in terms of a positive black identity.

Once he joins the Brotherhood, though, his new identity becomes increasingly distant from the meaning of his blackness. When the Black community begins to recognize him by his Brotherhood name, he thinks, "I am what they think I am." But at the same time he has begun to confront the meaning of being Black. He realizes the inadequacy of his ideological dismissal of Ras the Exhorter's black power arguments. He picks up physical symbols of the black man's image in America— pieces of his landlady's figurine of a grinning "red-lipped, wide-mouthed Negro"; a link of chain Brother Tarp filed off to escape the chain gang (a symbol of the Black man as criminal and slave); and one of the Sambo dolls Tod Clifton was selling when he was killed, tying together Clifton's degradation, the Negro as "mechanical man" operated by whites, and the protagonist himself, who is being manipulated by the Brotherhood for its own ends. Eventually all these things, along with his high school diploma and Brotherhood identity papers, find their way into the briefcase he was given on the night of the battle royal—the combined personal and historical racial identity he must carry with him.

With the killing of Tod Clifton the novel's images of blindness and invisibility coalesce. Realizing that Clifton was just one of thousands of Blacks who fell outside the scope of the Brotherhood's vision, the protagonist sees in Brother Jack's glass eye the real relationship between the Brotherhood and himself: blindness. And when he discovers Rinehartism, he recognizes how blind *he* has been to a whole dimension of reality, including his own invisibility. The world as seen through the eyes of Rinehart, the man of many identities, is the world as possibility, the rich world of Black life which is invisible to the eyes of the white Brothers.

The man who chooses himself, Kierkegaard writes, "discovers now that the self he chooses contains an endless multiplicity, inasmuch as it has a history, a history in which he acknowledges identity with himself" (*Either/Or*). This is exactly what happens to Ellison's protagonist as he recognizes and embraces his essential identity: "And now all past humiliations became precious parts of my experience, and for the first time . . . I began to accept my past. . . . I saw that they were more than separate experiences. They were me; they defined me." And since all these humiliations were a function of his invisibility in the eyes of whites, it is as an invisible man that he chooses himself: "So I'd accept it, I'd explore it, rine and heart."

But his acceptance is still not a full one, for he decides to use his invisibility as a mask. He will avenge himself on the Brotherhood by confirming all their misconceptions about Harlem and black people: "I'd overcome 'em with yeses, undermine 'em with grins, agree them to death and destruction." But in the midst of the Harlem riot it dawns on him that *he* has again been the dupe: "By pretending to agree I *had* indeed agreed, had made myself responsible . . ." It becomes clear for the first time that his grandfather's advice was the worst kind of collaboration, the most insidious treason. Rinehartism, like Bledsoism, will inevitably be at the expense of other Blacks. One is what one does, and it is impossible to act in a manner contrary to the self one has chosen to be.

—Jerry Wasserman, "Embracing the Negative: *Native Son* and *Invisible Man*," *Studies in American Fiction* 4, No. 1 (Spring 1976): 100–102

ROBERT E. ABRAMS ON THE DREAM WORLD OF THE INVISIBLE MAN

[Robert E. Abrams (b. 1943) is a professor of English at the University of Washington. In this extract, Abrams explores Ellison's use of dreams and subjectivity in *Invisible Man*, linking the work to Lewis Carroll's *Alice in Wonderland*.]

To peer down into the depths of dream in Ellison's novel, then, is to gaze into a contradictory and equivocating world reflecting back to waking reason what Melville terms "the mystery of human subjectivity," all "profounder emanations" from which "never unravel their own intricacies, and have no proper endings." Moreover, as *Invisible Man* progresses, all waking defenses against the oneiric universe give way. Ellison allows his protagonist no rational refuge from it. Unlike other dream-haunted figures in literature—unlike Dodgson's Alice, who can flee back into a tidy, well-regulated Victorian universe, unlike even De Quincey, who can claim that the "moral" of his hallucinatory "sufferings" is that the would-be opium-eater should be forewarned—Ellison's hero is left, at the close of the novel, without any standpoint beyond the incongruity and dissonance of dream towards which to flee from it and from which to judge it. As the novel advances, received moral and intellectual foundations all but collapse for Invisible Man, who sees through one tidy illusion of orderliness after another. Homer Barbee's envisagement of the modern black experience according to the biblical paradigm of the Promised Land and Brother Jack's rigid, pseudo-scientific dogmatism molt into an inscrutable world-in-itself "too obscure for learned classification, . . . too ambiguous for the most ambiguous words." Stepping "outside the narrow borders of what men call reality," Ellison's narrator discovers, beyond the "pattern" of human "certainties," an anarchic, absurd universe "without direction." His capacity to define and to judge finally breaks down completely, so that, in the Epilogue, "I condemn and affirm, say no and say yes, say yes and say no[,] . . . denounce and . . . defend." If there were the possibility of oracle in the bewildering, problematic universe of *Invisible Man,* that possibility might conceivably lie in dream, traditionally a fount of wisdom that transcends waking reason. But to descend into hallucinatory depths in Ellison's novel is to lose "one's sense of time completely," to see one's basic perceptional models shattered, to become immersed in a prevaricating, multidimensional world where the only governing principle is "ambivalence." Dreaming in *Invisible Man* is as anarchic as in Dodgson's *Alice's Adventures in Wonderland,* which has been explored as a revelation, via "dream-vision," of a fluid and paradoxical universe lurking "beneath the man-made groundwork of Western thought and convention."

Certainly, even in dream, ambiguous vision is resisted, tidiness and definition are sought. Ellison's hero, like Dodgson's, does not easily accommodate himself to the equivocating fluidity of oneiric experience. His hunger for deliverance from its perils, however, only delivers him to fiendish jokes and reversals in disorienting nightmares. These nightmares are generally presided over by the taunting figure of his grandfather, whose surreal ruses mock and confound earnest reason. Such surreal jokes offer important lessons in epistemology. They dramatize the dangers of assuming that phenomena are necessarily rational and that entities are closed and fixed in a finite and conclusive universe:

> That night I dreamed I was at a circus with him [fit dream-setting of prevaricating set-ups that lure and fool, of reversals and equivocations]. . . . He told me to open my brief case and read what was inside and I did, finding an official envelope stamped with the state seal; and inside the envelope I found another and another, endlessly, and I thought I would fall of weariness. . . . "Now open that one." And I did and in it I found an engraved document. . . . "Read it," my grandfather said. "Out loud!"
> "To Whom It May Concern," I intoned. "Keep This Nigger-Boy Running."
> I awoke with the old man's laughter ringing in my ears.

In keeping with the old man's equivocating deathbed utterance—a "constant puzzle" which, in its paradoxes and ambivalences, invites yet baffles interpretation, and seems deliberately designed to do so—the old man himself, in his grandson's innermost, oneiric consciousness, mocks reason with surreal irrationality. He proffers that gift of fluid, ever-ambivalent vision which, had waking Invisible Man initially accepted it, would have kept him from falling for those "official"-looking letters, written by Bledsoe, which actually keep him "running" for a time. In dream the principle of certitude itself is subverted, and thus that subspecies of certitude which allows equivocators to diddle dolts.

—Robert E. Abrams, "The Ambiguities of Dreaming in Ellison's *Invisible Man,*" *American Literature* 49, No. 4 (January 1978): 599–601

[J. T. Hansen is a professor of English at the University of Puget Sound. In this extract, Hansen explores the world of *Invisible Man* in the context of the black experience in America.]

Our interest in this discussion will be partly the features of Black culture which are directly affected by the dominant society and partly those which have been overlooked in the past, those which are indigenous to Black experience in America. The latter is what the Invisible Man calls "my past" versus the past which has been defined and directed by authority figures within the dominant society. He must learn to distinguish between his minority status and his cultural heritage.

Our line of inquiry begins by describing how the treatment of character from the picaresque tradition combines with anthropological findings in the definition of Black "lifestyles" in *Invisible Man*. These lifestyles have been investigated using the normative methods of the social sciences and are, on a quantitative basis, a very accurate description of Black experience in the aggregate. The novelist is interested in patterns of order, too, but fictional methods are dramatic rather that normative. The novelist draws upon the raw disorder of direct experience in order to dramatize the various kinds of influences involved in the life of the individual. The picaresque novel is noted for the scope of its social interests. The picaresque hero moves widely through society, partly to describe aspects of society the reader does not know and partly to provide the realistic detail necessary for a convincing dramatization. Combining these two approaches to the pattern of Black culture will enable us to observe both its quantitative and qualitative aspects. It will show the holistic relationship of social factors seen in general terms and in acutely specific terms from the perspective of one representative individual.

The picaresque treatment of character provides an ideal medium for presenting these relationships. The picaresque hero, who is not recognized as a member of any social group, simply makes his way through society seeking a place for himself. Luck and necessity, trial and error, determine his course often more than his own conscious desires or decisions. He is introduced to successive social groups by master or teacher figures. The hero is a student-apprentice who participates in the group's initiation procedures. Especially in novels which are fictional autobiography, the reader is given a thorough insight into his subjective responses.

The Invisible Man's geographical mobility takes him from the Deep South and north to Harlem. Socially, he moves from a southern town through a Black college and into the urban ghetto. Through this process, he meets and learns from two sets of master figures. The first set is readily acknowledged by the dominant society. He is urged to follow the lead of this group in order to find personal success and to improve the conditions of Black people. Bledsoe (the college president), Norton (the White trustee), Lucius Brockway (the skilled laborer), and Brother Jack (the political activist), all try and fail to convince him to accept their model of social identity. The second group is overlooked by the first, and it is difficult even for the hero to recognize them. It includes his grandfather (an Old South Black), the Vet from the Golden Day (an institutionalized social deviant), Mary Rambo (a ghetto Black), and Tod Clifton (a disillusioned activist). The second group has a solid sense of Black cultural heritage and thus exposes the hero to values which make it impossible for him to accept uncritically any of the social roles available through the dominant society.

Some anthropologists define the following lifestyles among Black Americans: Down Home, Mainstream, Street People, and Militant. Down Home refers to values and behaviors which reflect cultural roots in the South. Mainstream Blacks accept the primacy of Anglo-American values, develop professional careers available to Blacks, and have a sense of respectability. Street People are urban Blacks, usually in the North, whose lifestyles are influenced by conditions in the central city where unemployment, urban institutions, and extended family relationships are important. Militants react against conditions which they consider abusive and affirm Black pride, the uniqueness of their cultural heritage, and the necessity of confronting the White society which dominates their existence.

Johnetta B. Cole gives the following description of Down Home people:

This is the traditional way of Black folks. It is basically rural and southern. It centers in the kitchens of Black homes, in the church halls for suppers, in fraternal orders. Down Home is a common expression among Black Americans, indicating one's point of origin, down south, or the simple, decent way of life.

The Invisible Man was born and raised in the South and knew this lifestyle well. The Battle Royal illustrates the frustration and pain which Blacks must accept under the conditions of overt racism in the South. The dominant culture has the power to force them to degrade themselves in order to gain access to the resources they need if they are to experience success. Despite these frustrations, Down Home people developed a marvelous culture which only recently has been studied.

—J. T. Hansen, "A Holistic Approach to *Invisible Man*," *MELUS* 6, No. 1 (Spring 1979): 43–44

ROBERT G. O'MEALLY ON *INVISIBLE MAN* AND THE BLUES

[Robert G. O'Meally (b. 1948) is the director of African-American studies at Wesleyan University. He is the author of *Lady Day: The Many Faces of Billie Holliday* (1991) and *The Craft of Ralph Ellison* (1980), from which the following extract is taken. Here, O'Meally studies the influence of blues music on *Invisible Man*.]

Blues language and rhythms resound throughout *Invisible Man*. The novel begins and ends with reference to Louis Armstrong's blues. In the prologue, the narrator declares that, to compensate for his invisibility, he has strung his underground hole with 1369 light bulbs and, though he already owns one radio-phonograph, he wants four more in order to hear his favorite blues properly. In mock patriotic fashion, the narrator wants to eat his favorite dessert of vanilla ice cream (white) and sloe gin (red) while listening to Armstrong's plaintive blues, "What Did I Do To Be So Black and Blue?"

Armstrong's blues, improvised just a fraction behind and then ahead of the beat, seem to express something fundamental about the narrator's Afro-American sense of timing:

Invisibility, let me explain, gives one a slightly different sense of time, you're never quite on the beat. Sometimes you're ahead and sometimes behind. Instead of the swift and imperceptible flowing of time, you are aware of its nodes, those points where time stands still or from which it leaps ahead. And you slip into the breaks and look around. That's what you hear in Louis' music.

This lagging behind in time is in keeping with CPT (colored people's time), the old joke on "traditional" Afro-American lateness. The ability to slide artfully in and out of tempo, Ellison implies, also can be a weapon. The yokel of the prologue defeats the fast-footworking machine-timed boxer by simply stepping "inside of his opponent's sense of time."

In the prologue, Ellison indicates that by tuning into the most profound meanings of the blues one is put in touch with certain fundamental aspects of Afro-American history and culture. The Invisible Man stumbles awkwardly "in the spaces between the notes" of Armstrong's blues and "not only entered the music but descended, like Dante, into its depths." Deep between the beams of blues sound, he encounters a series of black folk forms: a spiritual, a folk story, a sermon, a blues-like moan. When he finally ascends from this strange "underworld of sound," he hears Louis Armstrong innocently state the theme of the novel, inquiring (in the words of the Fats Waller song): "What did I do/To be so black/And blue?"

The blues resound through many scenes in the first chapters of the novel. At times they seep almost imperceptibly into the action and increase its resonance by capturing the mood of the narrator. After departing from Rabb Hall (a stronghold of Brer Rabbit?), where Dr. Bledsoe tells our hero he has two days to pack his things and leave the dream campus, the Invisible Man wanders blankly across the school lawn, his stomach feeling achy. The blues, trailing in the distance, offer notes of sympathy: "From somewhere across the quiet of the campus the sound of an old guitar-blues plucked from an out-of-tune piano drifted toward me like a lazy, shimmering wave, like the echoed whistle of a lonely train, and my head went over again, against a tree this time, and I could hear it splattering the flowering vines."

Jim Trueblood's blues also prove soothing. They give eloquent and cathartic expression to his absurd situation (pointed out by some critics as an oedipal as well as existential crisis). Living on a country road far away from the "beautiful college" in an "old log cabin with its chinks filled with chalk-white clay," he tells his story over and over until he nearly sings it. Before his disgrace (he impregnated both his wife and his daughter), the college people occasionally had invited Trueblood to sing in the chapel for the white guests. But having brought shame upon "the whole race" by his misdeeds, Trueblood is the target of the college leaders' sharp hatred. Nonetheless, Trueblood manages to face up to his outrageously "blue" situation. Even after his wife has slashed him in the head, renounced and abandoned him, as well as marshaled community sentiment against him, Trueblood collects his strength and continues on courageously. He identifies with "the boss quail bird": "Like a good man, what he gotta do, he *do*." He also recalls his own heritage rooted in spirituals and the blues. Recounting the situation, Trueblood's speech achieves a kind of blues cadence:

> I thinks and thinks, until I thinks my brain go'n bust, 'bout how I'm guilty and how I ain't guilty. I don't eat nothin' and I don't drink nothin' and cain't sleep at night. Finally, one night, way early in the mornin', I looks up and sees the stars and I start singin'. I don't mean to, I didn't think 'bout it, just start singin'. I don't know what it was, some kinda church song, I guess. All I know is I *ends up* singin' the blues. I sings me some blues that night ain't never been sang before, and while I'm singin' them blues I makes up my mind that I ain't nobody but myself and ain't nothin' I can do but let whatever is gonna happen, happen.

In his solitude, after releasing "some kinda church song" that dissolves into a blues, the black sharecropper finds himself able to face his family and community with renewed strength. Somehow the blues provide just the vehicle for coming to terms with the twisted and painful details of Trueblood's situation; by expressing himself in this "near tragic, near lyric" form, he conquers his fearful guilt. In the presence of Norton, the white college trustee, the Invisible Man is "torn between humiliation and fascination" at the farmer's story. But our young and ambitious hero is more interested, at this juncture,

in winning a tip from Norton than in learning about the
strengths and mysteries of his culture.

—Robert G. O'Meally, *The Craft of Ralph Ellison* (Cambridge,
MA: Harvard University Press, 1980), pp. 85–87

RALPH ELLISON ON AFRICAN AMERICANS AND THE MILITARY

[Ralph Ellison, aside from writing fiction, was an astute
critic. His essays are found in *Shadow and Act* (1964)
and *Going to the Territory* (1986). In this extract from
an introduction to *Invisible Man* written in 1981, Ellison
eloquently discusses the role of African Americans in
the American military.]

The narrative that was upstaged by the voice which spoke so
knowingly of invisibility (pertinent here because it turned out to
have been a blundering step toward the present novel),
focused upon the experiences of a captured American pilot
who found himself in a Nazi prisoner-of-war camp in which he
was the officer of highest rank and thus by a convention of war
the designated spokesman for his fellow prisoners. Predictably,
the dramatic conflict arose from the fact that he was the only
Negro among the Americans, and the resulting racial tension
was exploited by the German camp commander for his own
amusement. Having to choose between his passionate rejection of both native and foreign racisms while upholding those
democratic values which he held in common with his white
countrymen, my pilot was forced to find support for his morale
in his sense of individual dignity and in his newly awakened
awareness of human loneliness. For him that war-born vision of
virile fraternity of which Malraux wrote so eloquently was not
forthcoming, and much to his surprise he found his only
justification for attempting to deal with his countrymen as
comrades-in-arms lay precisely in those old betrayed promises
proclaimed in such national slogans and turns-of-phrase as
those the hero of Hemingway's *A Farewell to Arms* has found
so obscene during the chaotic retreat from Caporetto. But

while Hemingway's hero managed to put the war behind him and opt for love, for my pilot there was neither escape nor a loved one waiting. Therefore he had either to affirm the transcendent ideals of democracy and his own dignity by aiding those who despised him, or accept his situation as hopelessly devoid of meaning; a choice tantamount to rejecting his own humanity. The crowning irony of all this lay in the fact that neither of his adversaries was aware of his inner struggle.

Undramatized, all this might sound a bit extreme, yet historically most of the nation's conflicts of arms have been—at least for Afro-Americans—wars-within-wars. Such was true of the Civil War, the last of the Indian Wars, of the Spanish American War, and of World Wars I and II. And in order for the Negro to fulfill his duty as a citizen it was often necessary that he fight for his self-affirmed right to fight. Accordingly, my pilot was prepared to make the ultimate wartime sacrifice that most governments demand of their able-bodied citizens, but his was one that regarded his life as of lesser value than the lives of whites making the same sacrifice. This reality made for an existential torture, which was given a further twist of the screw by his awareness that once the peace was signed, the German camp commander could immigrate to the United States and immediately take advantage of freedoms that were denied the most heroic of Negro servicemen. Thus democratic ideals and military valor alike were rendered absurd by the prevailing mystique of race and color.

I myself had chosen the merchant marine as a more democratic mode of service (as had a former colleague, a poet, who was lost off Murmansk on his first trip to sea), and as a seaman ashore in Europe I had been encountering numerous Negro soldiers who gave me vivid accounts of the less-than-democratic conditions under which they fought and labored. But having had a father who fought on San Juan Hill, in the Philippines and in China, I knew that such complaints grew out of what was then an archetypical American dilemma: How could you treat a Negro as equal in war and then deny him equality during times of peace? I also knew something of the trials of Negro airmen, who after being trained in segregated units and undergoing the abuse of white officers and civilians alike were prevented from flying combat missions.

Indeed, I had published a short story which dealt with such a situation, and it was in that attempt to convert experience into fiction that I discovered that its implicit drama was far more complex than I had assumed. For while I had conceived of it in terms of a black-white, majority-minority conflict, with white officers refusing to recognize the humanity of a Negro who saw mastering the highly technical skills of a pilot as a dignified way of serving his country while improving his economic status, I came to realize that my pilot was also experiencing difficulty in seeing *himself.* And this had to do with his ambivalence before his own group's divisions of class and diversities of culture; an ambivalence which was brought into focus after he crash-landed on a Southern plantation and found himself being aided by a Negro tenant farmer whose outlook and folkways were a painful reminder of his own tenuous military status and their common origin in slavery. A man of two worlds, my pilot felt himself to be misperceived in both and thus was at ease with neither. In brief, the story depicts his conscious struggle for self-definition and for an invulnerable support for his individual dignity. I by no means was aware of his relationship to the invisible man, but clearly he possessed some of the symptoms.

—Ralph Ellison, "Introduction" (1981), *Invisible Man* (New York: Modern Library, 1992), pp. xv–xviii

MIKE W. MARTIN ON FAITH, HUMAN NATURE, AND *INVISIBLE MAN*

[Mike W. Martin is a former professor at Chapman College in Orange, California. In this extract, Martin explores the Invisible Man's faith in the goodness of human nature and the results of his trusting disposition.]

With few exceptions, willing dupes do not, as the expression suggests, intend or will to be deceived, although they act much as if they did. Nor need they be intentional self-deceivers who have some sense of where the truth resides and then turn away out of fear, guilty, laziness, or whatever. They are willing—deliberately or tacitly—to allow someone else to guide their activities and reasoning, and they do desire to be led in the general direction the deceiver appears to be leading them. Often their naive trust in their guide is based on lack of intelligence, foolhardiness, or laziness. But sometimes, as with the protagonist, the causes are more interesting. The Invisible Man has two related motivating dispositions. First, he is overly confident of the purity of others' motives. In this respect he is like Captain Delano in Melville's *Benito Cereno* (from which Ellison took an epigraph for his novel). Both have unreasonable degrees of trust in the goodness of human nature. Second, this trust is accompanied by an unwillingness to assume personal responsibility for exercising autonomy in forming his own plans and beliefs. This is shown in his eagerness to submit to the de facto authority of both the Southern white system and Bledsoe, without examining the justification of that authority. It is shown also in his imitation of the life models of his parents, Bledsoe, Jack, and Rinehart without imaginatively seeking alternative possibilities rooted more firmly in his own experience.

As will be seen shortly, however, Ellison does not tie his moral appraisal of naiveté about the possibility of moral harm to any narrow set of motives. He seeks a more universal indictment of willing dupery where moral considerations are involved. The narrator's self indictment is a way of pointing to a wide variety of possible tragedies in allowing oneself to be misled and misused by an illusion and its propagator.

This general aim is clear from Ellison's portrayal of a world filled with innumerable "easy marks." White philanthropists like Norton are pleased by the false images President Bledsoe conveys. Bledsoe thrives on bleeding charity from whites by telling them "the kind of lie they want to hear." He states his cynicism baldly: "Why, the dumbest black bastard in the cotton patch knows that the only way to please a white man is to tell him a lie." Jack and the Marxist Brotherhood are equally manipulative in their deception of the Harlem community. Their apparent acts of concern are pretense designed to hide the way they use the community as raw material for attaining Brotherhood goals. Upon assigning him as chief spokesman of the Harlem District,

Jack gives the protagonist the recipe for demagoguery: "Say what the people want to hear, but say it in such a way that they'll do what we wish." Hambro, the Brotherhood's theoretician, later adds, "It's impossible *not* to take advantage of the people"; "the trick is to take advantage of them in their own best interest." And as the narrator comes to realize, the Harlem dwellers are willing dupes of con artists like the many-faced Rinehart, who alternately uses gambling, prostitution, and the role of Reverend ("Spiritual Technologist") to relieve the gullible of their pocketbooks.

In order to provide for sufficient generality, Ellison sets forth a profoundly moving moral allegory which centers on naiveté per se and makes motives a subordinate matter. The allegory, to which we can now turn, is the Jim Trueblood tale of incest.
—Mike W. Martin, "*Invisible Man* and the Indictment of Innocence," *CLA Journal* 25, No. 3 (March 1982): 293–95

KERRY MCSWEENEY ON *INVISIBLE MAN* AND *MIDDLEMARCH*

[Kerry McSweeney is a professor of English at McGill University in Montreal, Canada, and the author of *Tennyson and Swinburne as Romantic Naturalists* (1981), *Four Contemporary Novelists* (1983), and *George Eliot: A Literary Life* (1991). In this extract from her study of *Invisible Man,* McSweeney finds *Invisible Man* to be following in the British novelistic tradition (especially that of George Eliot's *Middlemarch*) in its complex presentation of social and moral themes.]

The big questions for the American novelist, as Ellison eloquently phrased them in 1957, were these:

> How does one in the novel (the novel which is a work of art and not a disguised piece of sociology) persuade the American reader to identify that which is basic in man beyond all differences of class, race, wealth, or formal education? . . . How does one persuade readers with the least knowledge of literature to

recognize the broader values implicit in their lives? How, in a word, do we affirm that which *is* stable in human life beyond all despite all processes of social change? How give the reader that which we do have in abundance, all the countless untold and wonderful variations on the themes of identity and freedom and necessity, love and death, and with all the mystery of personality undergoing its endless metamorphosis?

There is nothing new about these criteria for assessing a novel, nor about Ellison's ambitions as a writer of prose fiction. Both are squarely in the great moralizing tradition of the realistic novel. Ellisons's claims, for example, are essentially the same as those made by George Eliot in England in the middle of the nineteenth century when she spoke of "the greatest benefit we owe the artist [being] the extension of our sympathies. Appeals founded on generalizations and statistics [i.e., on sociology] require a sympathy ready made, a moral sentiment already in activity; but a picture of human life such as a great artist can give, surprises [readers] into that attention to what is apart from themselves, which may be called the raw material of moral sentiment. [Art] is a mode of amplifying experience." In realizing their intentions, both the author of *Invisible Man* and the author of *Middlemarch* use the same general strategy of blending their directly expressed thematic concerns and moral propositions with a densely textured, solidly specified, and vividly presented social world. Many are the variations played in *Invisible Man* on the themes of identity, freedom, and the mystery of personality; but they are no less central to the novel than is the manifold of wonderfully rendered aural and visual particulars: for example, the voices of Trueblood recalling his sweet nights in Mobile, Peter Wheatstraw singing about his woman, and Ras exhorting a mob; or the descriptions of the types who frequent the lobby of the Men's House, of the crowd at Tod Clifton's funeral, and of the clutter of household objects of the dispossessed couple, including the paragraph-long description of the spilled contents of a single drawer that the narrator picks up from the snow.

While the mixture of moral concern and felt life in *Invisible Man* is traditional, the formal means employed to shape and organize the material are modernist. In the artistic elaboration and presentation of its subjects, and in the degree of formal control employed, Ellison's novel has more in common with Joyce's *Ulysses* than with Eliot's *Middlemarch*. These elaboration's include the patterns formed by recurring images, symbols, and motifs; the polyphonic organization of chapters, some of which have a realistic or narrative level; the changes from chapter to chapter (and even within a single chapter) in style and presentational mode—from straightforwardly representational to expressionistic and surrealistic; and the intermittent use of techniques of defamiliarization (like the eruption of Jack's glass eye) and other devices that complicate the reader's engagement with the text. 〈. . .〉 one may say that one of the most striking and original features of *Invisible Man* is the counterpoint between a compelling story that is in its own right startlingly and sometimes horrifyingly eventful (there are no battle royals, police shootings, or race riots in *Ulysses*) and the high degree of artistic elaboration, which repeatedly invites the reader to reflect rather than to react.

—Kerry McSweeney, Invisible Man: *Race and Identity* (Boston: Twayne, 1988), pp. 11–13

STEVEN C. TRACY ON PEETIE WHEATSTRAW AND TRUEBLOOD

[Steven C. Tracy (b. 1954) is the author of *Langston Hughes and the Blues* (1988) and *Going to Cincinnati: A History of the Blues in the Queen City* (1993). In this extract, Tracy compares the roles of Peetie Wheatstraw and Trueblood in *Invisible Man,* finding that Wheatstraw is an energetic, vibrant character while Trueblood is resigned and passive.]

〈. . .〉 the character of Peetie Wheatstraw in the book is much like Paul Garon described the blues singer and his use of the name—he is "a protest against the drab role the black man was supposed to fill, but also a striking representation of what the future might hold." But his protest and his representation of the future are both firmly rooted in tradition. William Bunch recorded a song in 1941 entitled "Seeing is Believing" that states, in essence, what the protagonist comes to realize in the novel both in medium and message. To the musical accompaniment of a twelve bar blues, Peetie sings,

> The world is all right, it is the people
> that makes it bad (x2)
> You been believing everything you hear,
> ooh, well, well it's no wonder you feel
> so sad.

It is certainly no coincidence that later, during the riot, there are a number of connections between that scene and the scene with Wheatstraw. The protagonist is drawn into this scene by a reference to "dog days," which he doesn't understand here either. In this case, though, the rioters seem to have "got the dog." They are acting, "picking it clean" as they go along, echoing the song that comes to the protagonist's mind after he departs from Peetie's presence and receives his shocking news from Emerson's son. These things, the presence of a singer whose voice had a "blues singer's timbre," and the actions of the people to subvert the old, inoperable plans that shoved them into their tenement all draw the parallel between . Wheatstraw's section and theirs. Both sections provide examples of responses to the system and attitudes fostered by it, demonstrating that responses are possible.

Wheatstraw is certainly a more positive figure than the other major blues singer of the text, Trueblood. Having committed incest with his daughter at the climax of a dream in which he has violated a number of Southern social taboos and finds himself in bed with a white woman, Trueblood works out his problem while he is singing the blues:

> . . . and while I'm singin' them blues I makes up my mind that I ain't nobody but myself and ain't nothin' I can do but let whatever is gonna happen, happen.

While it is significant and appropriate that Trueblood realizes and accepts both his identity and individuality while performing in the folklore tradition of his people, his resignation to his fate makes him a passive victim of what he perceives as his limitations. In this he not only affirms a sexual stereotype created by whites and forced upon Blacks, but he also turns his life-giving act into a violent act and the creative act (his story-telling) into a degrading, economically-motivated act. Whether or not he reflects the similar corruption of Norton or represents fertility in the face of sterility of those Blacks in the college and asylum on either side of him, he is certainly not "representative" of anything that Norton or those in the college try to make him. He is a weak and pitiful man whose blues are a self-serving rationalization of his weakness.

Wheatstraw does not degrade himself for money and goods; Wheatstraw does not identify himself in such negative terms as "nobody but myself." He is energetic, bursting with personality and group identity. He has perhaps found what Ellison's nameless protagonist is looking for: a way of being himself with integrity in a hostile world. Wheatstraw has not, of course, solved the problem of how to gain political power or achieve equality in the eyes of his "bosses." But then, with his powerful imagination and wit, to gain equality would be to lose. The economic, legal, and social problems the protagonist wants solved are to be solved by a change in attitude, beginning with an acceptance, by Blacks and Whites, of a Peetie Wheatstraw. Like the speaker in Langston Hughes's "I Too," one day people will see how beautiful he is, and be ashamed. Some people are, of course, ashamed of Trueblood, but only because, unlike Wheatstraw, he loved himself better than he loved his baby. Wheatstraw is less concerned with directly challenging or violating White Southern codes than he is with existing outside and above them. That way he avoids as much as possible being controlled by them. This is the presence of folklore in its most positive sentence, representing *possibilities* rather than *limitations* of Trueblood.

If the search for identity is *the* American theme, as Ellison said it is in his *Paris Review* interview, the real-life Peetie Wheatstraw, as model for the fictional Peetie Wheatstraw, provided an excellent example of a person who had grappled with the issues and advantages related to personal identity. William Bunch created a persona that was highly traditional, with its roots in African-American folklore, and individualistic and original as well. Peetie Wheatstraw was not so much a mask for him as it was a broader identity, one that placed him in an historical, social and cultural milieu and sharply defined both individual and generic characteristics. It was Bunch's way of expressing his faith and trust in his own experience and his own definition of reality, affirming the principles of individual freedom while drawing upon the strength of group traditions.

—Steven C. Tracy, "The Devil's Son-in-Law and *Invisible Man*," *MELUS* 15, No. 3 (Fall 1988): 61–63

KALU OGBAA ON *INVISIBLE MAN* AND *HEART OF DARKNESS*

[Kalu Ogbaa (b. 1945) is a professor of English at Southern Connecticut University and the author of *Gods, Oracles, and Divination: Folkways in China Achebe's Novels* (1992) and *The Gong and the Flute: African Literacy Development and Celebration* (1994). In this extract, Ogbaa compares Ellison's novel with Joseph Conrad's *Heart of Darkness*.

The invisibility of the Invisible Man and the experience and knowledge of other people's cultures and traditions by Ellison are important qualifications of a novelist and his folk hero who want to play the role of spokesman and teacher. In fact, it has been argued very persuasively that *Invisible Man* compares very favorably with Conrad's *Heart of Darkness*:

> In the epilogue to *Invisible Man*, the narrator speaks of the "heart of darkness" of the South and he also speaks of his own "disembodied voice." It is obvious throughout the novel that Ellison has been influenced by numerous authors and that he uses many of their ideas. The preface quotes from Melville and Eliot, and other references to Emerson, and even Sartre, show that Ellison is a well-read man. And after discovering the Conrad references in the Epilogue, it becomes clear that *Invisible Man* and *Heart of Darkness* have much in common, even though one book is written by a twentieth-century black American and the other by a nineteenth-century white European. ⟨C. K. Hillegass⟩

Both novels also share much in theme and symbol. They deal with a jungle: *Heart of Darkness* with the "jungle of the Congo," and *Invisible Man* with the "jungle of Harlem." They both deal with the so-called good men who are "bearers of the white man's burden," a term meaning in practical terms the subjugation of black men, either in Africa or Harlem, a subjugation that results in great cruelty in the actions of one group of men toward the other group. In one novel, the white oppressors are Europeans who are "civilizing the "darker" continent of Africa, and in the other, the white oppressors are people like Mr. Norton, a man imbued with the "great tradition" of America, who, nonetheless, hinders the black man's development.

What the Invisible Man goes through is man's inhumanity to man and the oppression of a group of people by another. Such groups are not necessarily homogeneous by race but by a common intent to acquire power, authority, and money so as to use them on others—the theory of the big fish eating the small fish in order to get bigger. But such a discovery cannot be made by a folk hero like Bigger, who does not have the capacity to think or meditate on issues and incidents around him. His only capacity is creating violence without knowing how to avoid its consequences. Such a hero can hardly inspire his people with a vision that would help them transcend their historical dilemma. No, his noisy and violent life-style would not permit him to think and plan.

On the other hand, the Invisible Man goes underground after he has undertaken journeys of the soul which lead to an understanding of man's nature and identity. The hell-like cellar of outer Harlem provides a perfect solitude which is necessary for meditation, self-soul examination, and creativity. It is there that he removes his blindfolds so he can ascend to light again. So *Invisible Man* deals with man's blindness and the lifelong attempt of a man to throw off his blindfolds in order to see life as it is. The Invisible Man's quest for identity becomes Ellison's recipe recommended to all Americans of different racial extractions for fighting racial prejudice and bigotry, which are mainly due to ignorance, apathy and mental laziness.

—Kalu Ogbaa, "Protest and the Individual Talents of Three Black Novelists," *CLA Journal* 35, No. 2 (December 1991): 178–80

[Kun Jong Lee wrote "Ellison's *Invisible Man:*
Emersonianism Revised" as part of his doctoral disser-
tation, "Reading Race (in)to the American Renaissance:
A Study of Race in Emerson, Whitman, Melville, and
Ellison," for the University of Texas. In this extract from
that article, Lee explores the role of the grandfather in
Invisible Man and relates some of the novel's central
ideas to those found in the work of Emerson.]

The grandfather is more a representative voice of the African
American experience than a lineal ancestor of the nameless
hero, since his seemingly paradoxical deathbed advice encap-
sulates the gist of the African American vernacular wisdom for
"puttin' on massa." His survival strategy is, Ellison explains, "a
kind of jiujitsu of the spirit, a denial and rejection through
agreement." In jiujitsu, one of the basic principles is not to be
sucked up into the rhythm of the opponent's pace. Hence the
importance of maintaining one's own identity in the struggle
between cultural forces. The grandfather's injunction, then, may
be translated into a warning against "trying to be Paul"—
against the double consciousness that will make the hero "keep
running." Only at the end of his nightmarish odyssey, however,
does the nameless hero learn the significance of his grandfather's advice, although in the narrator's dreams and subcon-
scious his grandfather keeps asking to be read correctly while
sardonically watching him run. In fact, the grandfather is an
indispensable, though invisible, figure in the development of
the narrative: the narrative proper begins with his sphinxlike
advice and ends with his grandson's decoding of its message.
Thus the plot of the novel evolves around the advice: the protagonist's frightened flight from, blind reading of, and creative
acceptance of it. At first, the hero avoids the advice as if it
were a "curse." He associates it with something negative and
destructive: "the malicious, arguing part; the dissenting voice,
my grandfather part; the cynical, disbelieving part—the traitor
self that always threatened internal discord." Later, he follows it
literally in his anger against the Brotherhood, a strategy that
ends in fiasco. The irony of this episode is that his blind yessing
comes to choke himself rather than to undermine the brothers.

Finally, after recognizing "the hole" he inhabits in America, he realizes the absurdity of his own involvement in his society's effort to make him invisible. This realization makes him comprehend why meekness means treachery and how an African American can "find transcendence" in a racist society. The invisible protagonist now understands that the cryptic meaning of his grandfather's instruction is in essence to affirm the principle while denouncing its corruptions and corruptors.

The invisible man's interpretation of his grandfather's precept echoes Ellison's persistent argument that the principle of the American "sacred" documents should be respected notwithstanding its past distortions and appropriations. This echo also points toward three other affiliations linking Ellison, his literary namesake, and the key figures in his novel: these mirrorings connect Emerson with the grandfather, Emersonianism with the grandfather's advice, and Ellison with the protagonist. The association of Emerson with the grandfather has been suggested significantly by Ellison himself, who confesses that Emerson is "as difficult to pin down as the narrator's grandfather." Emerson and the grandfather are omnipresent, powerful voices of the past. They are ideological twins in that both celebrate an individual's identity as a revolutionary anchor. But their teachings are ambiguous and apt to be illusory or misleading; both are not universalistic but limited in their applications. One reason for the ambiguity and limitation is a self-deconstructing element in each teaching: racism for Emerson and spite for the grandfather. So both need to be read creatively, in an Emersonian sense.

Ellison's response to Emersonianism enacts a creative reading of the grandfather's advice: Ellison yesses it to death (in an ironic version of the affirmative Emersonian position) until Emersonianism chokes on him. In this way, like the narrator who reclaims his grandfather as his ancestor, Ellison brings Emerson into his own genealogy while subverting and expanding Emersonianism in the process: as the narrator reads his grandfather's advice while negating its (and his) anger and bitterness, so Ellison affirms the basic ideas of Emersonianism while neutralizing its negative aspect, resocializing its spiritualized, abstract premises, and reinterpreting its monologic, dogmatic, and oracular implications. Thus Ellison both accepts and rejects Emersonianism. This stance, paradoxically, makes him a truer American scholar in the Emersonian tradition, which, by its internal logic, asks for critique and reinterpretation in each age.

—Kun Jong Lee, "Ellison's *Invisible Man:* Emersonianism Revised," *PMLA* 107, No. 2 (March 1992) : 341–42

PHILIP GOULD ON RAS AND THE BROTHERHOOD

[Philip Gould (b. 1925) is a freelance writer, journalist, novelist, critic, and reviewer. In this extract, Gould studies the nature and function of Ras and the Brotherhood in *Invisible Man*, linking it with the notion of Pan-Africanism.]

Ras' first of two appearances in the novel temporarily invalidate the Brotherhood's depiction of him as the Destroyer, since, if nothing else, he shows mercy for a true "brother." A close look at Ras' exhortation shows that the central point on which it converges is practical necessity the essential importance of the economics of race. Beneath a CHECKS CASHED HERE sign, the Exhorter takes up this issue:

> "This is *Harlem*. This is *my* territory, the *black* mahn's territory. You think we let white folks come in like they come and spread their poison? Let 'em come in like they come and take over the numbers racket? Like they have all the stores? Talk sense, mahn, if you talking to Ras, talk sense."
>
> "This is sense," I said, "and you listened as we listened to you. . . . We'll be out here and the next time you go after one of our brothers with a knife—and I mean white or black—well, we won't forget it."

Invisible Man's retort, "This is sense," exploits the Ellisonian ambivalence of the word. "This" simultaneously harkens back to Ras' lesson in economic nationalism and seques into Invisible Man's threat. But the threat itself rhetorically subverts its own authority, for Invisible Man parrots Jack's definition of "brother," which Ellison earlier mocked during Invisible Man's first encounter with the white father. "All men who want a brotherly world," the young convert mechanically mimics, further exposing his loss of race-consciousness. By default Invisible Man unwittingly acknowledges the "sense" of Ras' plea.

In Ras' first appearance in *Invisible Man*, then, the "sense" of pan-Africanism actually occupies the narrower sphere of economic nationalism, and in this respect the Exhorter's words contain within them ideas from W. E. B. Du Bois' autobiography, *Dusk of Dawn*. In 1940 Du Bois endorsed the model of the "African communal group" where "ties of family and blood, mother and child, of group relationship, made the group leadership strong. . . . Here [in America] in subtle but real ways the communalism of the African clan can be transferred to the Negro American group." Further, Du Bois argues that blacks must take control of black art, "not to amuse the white audience, but to inspire and direct the acting Negro group itself." Because "most whites want Negroes to amuse them" and "demand caricature," it is necessary to organize a black artistic movement which is "deliberately planned." In *Dusk of Dawn* the idea of economic nationalism and resentment of white artistic patronage are thus yoked together—just as they are in *Invisible Man* when Ras mocks the two young black leftists by telling them to walk off the Brotherhood's white stage: " 'You young, don't play so cheap mahn.' " In 1947 Du Bois had asked an African-American audience, "How far will these young Negroes consider that their primary duty is toward the cultural group which they represent and which created them?" Disgusted with the new, white patron of Harlem, the composite effect of Ras' exhortation in the alley raises Du Bois' question again.

But Ras' claim that Harlem is "*his* territory" foreshadows the invalidation of pan-Africanism. In Ras' self-interestedness lies Ellison's well-known discomfort with the notion of African identity for American Negroes in general and himself in particular. After employing Ras to effect Tod's and Invisible Man's liberation from the Brotherhood, Ellison changes his *persona* in the script: the next time he appears he is "Ras the Exhorter become Ras the Destroyer." This "new Ras" in a different "costume" is Ellison's artificial creation, a disjointed caricature of a former character. Now in his public pose, masked with fur cap, shield, the cape of some wild animal's skin, the "Abyssinian chieftain" becomes a parody of the merciless African ruler sentencing the hero to death: " 'Ignore his lying tongue . . . Hang him up to teach the black people a lesson.' " After Invisible Man's climatic meditation on the world's blindness and his own invisibility, he throws the spear through Ras that "locked his jaws," thus obliterating the text's voice for pan-African leadership and identity. At the moment of silencing that voice, Invisible Man thinks that "it was as though for a moment I had surrendered my life and begun to live again."

—Philip Gould, "Ralph Ellison's 'Time-Haunted' Novel," *Arizona Quarterly* 49, No. 1 (Spring 1993): 129–31

Books by
Ralph Ellison

Invisible Man. 1952.

The Writer's Experience. (with Karl Shapiro). 1964.

Shadow and Act. 1964.

The City in Crisis (with Whitney M. Young, Jr., and Herbert Gans). 1967.

Going to the Territory. 1986.

Works about Ralph Ellison and Invisible Man

Alter, Robert. "The Apocalyptic Temper." *Commentary* 41, No. 6 (June 1966): 61–66.

Baker, Houston A., Jr. "To Move without Moving: An Analysis of Creativity and Commerce in Ralph Ellison's Trueblood Episode." *PMLA* 98 (1983): 828–45.

Benston, Kimberly, ed. *Speaking for You: The Vision of Ralph Ellison.* Washington, DC: Howard University Press, 1987.

Bloom, Harold, ed. *Ralph Ellison.* New York: Chelsea House, 1986.

Blount, Marcellus. " 'A Certain Eloquence': Ralph Ellison and the Afro-American Artist." *American Literary History* 1 (1989): 675–88.

Busby, Mark. *Ralph Ellison.* Boston: Twayne, 1991.

Butler, Robert J. "Dante's *Inferno* and Ellison's *Invisible Man:* A Study in Literary Continuity." *CLA Journal* 28 (1984): 57–77.

———. "Patterns of Movement in Ellison's *Invisible Man.*" *American Studies* 21 (1980): 5–21.

Butler, Thorpe. "What Is to Be Done? Illusion, Identity, and Action in Ralph Ellison's *Invisible Man.*" *CLA Journal* 27 (1984): 315–31.

Cheshire, Ardner R., Jr. "*Invisible Man* and the Life of Dialogue." *CLA Journal* 20 (1976): 19–34.

Chester, Alfred, and Vilma Howard. "The Art of Fiction VIII: Ralph Ellison." *Paris Review* No. 8 (Spring 1955): 55–71.

Christian, Barbara. "Ralph Ellison: A Critical Study." In *Black Expression,* ed. Addison Gayle, Jr. New York: Weybright & Talley, 1969, pp. 353–65.

Fabre, Michel. "The Narrator/Narratee Relationship in *Invisible Man.*" *Callaloo* 8 (1985): 535–43.

Finholt, Richard. "Ellison's Chattering-Monkey Blues." In Filholt's *American Visionary Fiction: Mad Metaphysics as Salvation Psychology*. Port Washington, NY: Kennikat Press, 1978, pp. 96–111.

Gross, Theodore L. *The Heroic Ideal in American Literature.* New York: Oxford University Press, 1971.

Harper, Phillip Brian. " 'To Become One and Yet Many': Psychic Fragmentation and Aesthetic Synthesis in Ralph Ellison's *Invisible Man.*" *Black American Literature Forum* 23 (1989): 681–700.

Helmling, Steven. "T. S. Eliot and Ralph Ellison: Insiders, Outsiders, and Cultural Authority." *Southern Review* 25 (1989): 841–58.

Kostelanetz, Richard. *Politics in the African-American Novel: James Weldon Johnson, W. E. B. Du Bois, Richard Wright, and Ralph Ellison.* Westport, CT: Greenwood Press, 1991.

List, Robert N. *Dedalus in Harlem: The Joyce-Ellison Connection.* Washington, DC: University Press of America, 1982.

Lyne, William. "The Signifying Modernist: Ralph Ellison and the Limits of the Double Consciousness." *PMLA* 107 (1992): 319–30.

Lyons, Eleanor. "Ellison and the Twentieth-Century American Scholar." *Studies in American Fiction* 17 (1989): 93–106.

Marx, Stephen. "Beyond Hibernation: Ralph Ellison's 1982 Version of *Invisible Man.*" *Black American Literature Forum* 23 (1989): 701–21.

Nadel, Alan. *Invisible Criticism: Ralph Ellison and the American Canon.* Iowa City: University of Iowa Press, 1988.

O'Meally, Robert G., ed. *New Essays on* Invisible Man. Cambridge: Cambridge University Press, 1988.

Ostendorf, Berndt. *Black Literature in White America.* Brighton, UK: Harvester Press, 1982.

Reed, Brian K. "The Iron and the Flesh: History as Machine in Ellison's *Invisible Man.*" *CLA Journal* 37 (1994): 261–73.

Sanders, Archie D. "Odysseus in Black." *CLA Journal* 13 (1970): 217–28.

Saunders, Catherine E. "Makers or Bearers of Meaning? Sex and the Struggle for Self-Definition in Ralph Ellison's *Invisible Man*." *Critical Matrix* 5 (1989): 1–28.

Schor, Edith. *Visible Ellison: A Study of Ralph Ellison's Fiction*. Westport, CT: Greenwood Press, 1993.

Scott, Nathan A., Jr. "Ralph Ellison's Vision of Communitas." In *American Writing Today,* ed. Richard Kostelanetz. Troy, NY: Whitston, 1991, pp. 103–13.

Stanford, Ann Folwell. "He Speaks for Whom? Inscription and Reinscription of Women in *Invisible Man* and *The Salt Eaters*." *MELUS* 18, No. 2 (Summer 1992): 17–31.

Tewarie, Bhoendradatt. "Southern Elements in Ellison's *Invisible Man*." *Journal of General Education* 35 (1983): 189–200.

Urgo, Joseph R. *Novel Frames: Literature as Guide to Race, Sex, and History in American Culture*. Jackson: University of Mississippi Press, 1991.

Walker, James. "What Do You Say Now, Ralph Ellison?" *Black Creation* 1 (1970): 16–18.

Warren, Robert Penn. "The Unity of Experience." *Commentary* 39, No. 5 (May 1965): 91–96.

Watts, Jerry Gafio. *Heroism and the Black Intellectual: Ralph Ellison, Politics, and Afro-American Intellectual Life*. Chapel Hill: University of North Carolina Press, 1994.

Weber, Daniel B. "Metropolitan Freedom and Restraint in Ellison's *Invisible Man*." *College Literature* 12 (1985): 163–75.

Winther, Per. "The Ending of Ralph Ellison's *Invisible Man*." *CLA Journal* 25 (1981): 162–81.

Wright, John S. "To the Battle Royal: Ralph Ellison and the Quest for Black Leadership in Postwar America." In *Recasting America: Culture and Politics in the Age of the Cold War,* ed. Larry May. Chicago: University of Chicago Press, 1989, pp. 246–66.

Wynter, Sylvia. "On Disenchanting Discourse: 'Minority' Literary Criticism and Beyond." *Cultural Critique* 7 (1987): 207–44.

Index of
Themes and Ideas